SWEET SOULFUL BAKING

SWEET SOULFUL BAKING

RECIPES INSPIRED BY
SOUTHERN ROOTS

MONIQUE
McLEOD–POLANCO
CREATOR OF PEACHES 2 PEACHES

PAGE STREET
PUBLISHING CO.

PAGE STREET
PUBLISHING CO.

First published in 2023 by

Page Street Publishing Co.

27 Congress Street, Suite 1511

Salem, MA 01970

www.pagestreetpublishing.com

Distributed by Macmillan, sales in Canada by The Canadian Manda Group.

27 26 25 24 23   1 2 3 4 5

ISBN-13: 978-1-64567-922-6

ISBN-10: 1-64567-922-5

Library of Congress Control Number: 2022950269

Cover and book design by Meg Baskis for Page Street Publishing Co.

Photography by Monique McLeod-Polanco

Printed and bound in the United States of America

MATERNAL GRANDMOTHER, ANNIE LOUISE.
MY LOVE FOR BAKING WOULD NOT EXIST
WITHOUT HER LOVE AND INFLUENCE.

CONTENTS

INTRODUCTION

Desserts have always been a huge part of all my family celebrations. Whether it was a birthday, graduation, Thanksgiving or Christmas, desserts were at the center and everyone had a favorite. This book is filled with delicious recipes inspired by my childhood, my family and my favorite desserts that I have acquired throughout my lifetime.

I am a true New Yorker. I was born in Manhattan and raised in the Bronx, but my roots are from the South. My mother was born in St. Augustine, Florida. It is the oldest city in America, rich in history and culture, and it is the city where my grandfather's first cousin, Lennette, owned a luncheonette Dr. Martin Luther King Jr. frequented during the civil rights movement. It is also the city with beautiful brick streets, the historical Castillo de San Marco, the Fountain of Youth, Fort Mose Historic State Park and the oldest wooden schoolhouse.

Growing up, I spent all my summers there. Since my mom was a teacher, as soon as school ended for the year, we were in the car driving down south to start an amazing summer at my grandmother's house, playing with my cousins and being in my happy place. When I tell people that my family is from Florida, they always say that Florida isn't really "down south." When they think of Florida, they think of South Beach Miami and Walt Disney World, the tourist areas. But most parts of Florida are very "southern" with southern accents and a lot of historic southern foods.

My great-grandmother was a pastry chef in St. Augustine, baking for some of the great pastry shoppes. My grandmother got her love of baking from her. She didn't bake professionally, but would always bake for all the family functions. My grandfather's mother regularly baked sweet potato pies for church functions and my grandfather worked in a bakery on the boardwalk in Asbury Park, New Jersey, and was a cook at several restaurants until he retired. Cooking and baking has been in my blood going generations back.

My grandparents moved to the North when my mother was nine years old. So, even though we were in New York, our food was rich in southern culture. Smothered pork chops, collard greens with ham hock, lima beans, black-eyed peas, buttermilk biscuits, grits and country ham were on the menu regularly.

And our desserts were *definitely* southern inspired. On Thanksgiving, we always had sweet potato pie, apple pie and pound cake. On Christmas, it was rum cake and bread pudding. And on Easter, it was always my grandmother's peach cobbler. Her pound cake was made for each and every holiday, regardless of the time of the year. We just knew if it was a holiday, there would be pound cake.

Growing up, I was always in the kitchen with my grandmother and mother, but I started experimenting with cooking and baking when I was about eight years old. Creating dishes and desserts fascinated me. I wanted to do what the adults were doing in the kitchen. However, I didn't go this route as a career path.

I went to Hunter College in NYC for my undergraduate, majoring in sociology, and I later attended Fordham University, graduating with a master's degree in social work. I worked for several years as a high school social worker in the Bronx. Whenever we had staff celebrations or events, I always baked the desserts. Brownies were always the number one request. Often people would tell me that I should open a bakery or a cafe. When my daughter was a baby, I decided to start posting some of the foods I made on social media, and I also created a blog called Peaches 2 Peaches. One of my pictures got the attention of the former talk show *The Chew*, and they asked if I would be a judge for an upcoming episode! It was definitely a career highlight. Eventually, I started getting paid sponsorships with food brands, so I created an LLC and officially started my business in food photography. This led to writing this book, which was a complete dream come true!

In this book, you'll find recipes that can be made for all types of celebrations, whether it's for family events, potlucks or milestone festivities. These are recipes inspired and created from family recipes and desserts I have had throughout the years. The chapters are divided into home baker–friendly sections like how to make desserts ahead of time, how to make desserts when you have no time and bite-sized desserts—all meant to make your baking and decorating easy to execute! Many have simple decor or tools to assist in making the most beautiful and delicious desserts.

Cooking and baking have always been my passions. I put all of my heart and soul into this book to create recipes you will love. So, turn the page, and let's start baking!

Monique McLeod-Polanco

SHOW STOPPING CAKES

CAKES HAVE ALWAYS BEEN A PART OF EVERY CELEBRATION IN MY FAMILY—birthdays, holidays, graduations, even family reunions. When there's something to celebrate, the cakes would come out.

When a birthday cake was made, it was basically just the cake layers and frosting. Back then, it was more about the taste than the look and they really were delicious!

As I got older and started baking myself, I started trying to decorate my cakes. I remember when I was a teenager, I made holiday-themed cakes. On Easter, I would shape my cake like an egg and decorate it with Easter colors and designs. And on Christmas, I would use red and green frosting while adding rosemary to look like pine. Baking and cake decorating became so fun.

You don't have to go to pastry or culinary school to be able to make beautifully decorated cakes. Creating a gorgeous cake for celebrations can be made simple by just adding a little something extra to them.

The cakes in this chapter include layer cakes decorated with lovely fresh flowers, like the Peaches & Cream Cake (page 22). Then, there are cakes decorated with a simple stencil and buttercream designs, like the Butter Pecan Cake with Browned Butter Cream Cheese Frosting (page 15). Each of these cakes will easily be a "showstopper" at any celebration.

BUTTER PECAN CAKE WITH BROWNED BUTTER CREAM CHEESE FROSTING

Growing up, the one staple we always had in our freezer was ice cream. My mom loves ice cream, so it is something that always needed to be on hand, and her favorite has always been creamy, rich butter pecan. Even if we got ice cream out, butter pecan was her go-to. There was no trying one of the other 30 flavors at Baskin-Robbins for something different. Once in a while, she would enjoy vanilla with other desserts, but butter pecan would be the number one choice. So, this flavorful cake is dedicated to my mother's favorite ice cream flavor.

SERVINGS: 10

BROWNED BUTTER
½ cup (114 g) unsalted butter, room temperature

PECANS
1 cup (109 g) pecans, chopped
2 tbsp (30 ml) melted butter

CAKE
3 large eggs, room temperature
½ cup (100 g) granulated sugar
1 cup (220 g) light brown sugar
¼ cup (57 g) butter, room temperature
⅔ cup (160 ml) vegetable oil
2 tsp (10 ml) vanilla extract
1 tbsp (15 ml) butter pecan extract
½ tsp butter extract, optional
1 cup (240 ml) sour cream, room temperature
½ cup (120 ml) buttermilk, room temperature
1 tbsp (14 g) baking powder
½ tsp baking soda
½ tsp salt
2½ cups (313 g) all-purpose flour

FOR THE BROWNED BUTTER: Cut the butter into pieces, add it to a small saucepan and melt it over medium heat, stirring occasionally. After it's melted, the butter will start to foam. After 5 to 7 more minutes, the milk solids will begin to brown. Once it is completely browned, immediately remove the butter from the heat and pour it into a small heatproof bowl. Refrigerate for 20 to 30 minutes or until it is semi-solid and the consistency of softened butter.

FOR THE PECANS: Preheat the oven to 350°F (177°C) and line a baking sheet with parchment paper.

Add the pecans and melted butter to a small bowl. Stir to fully coat the pecans. Spread the pecans out on the prepared baking sheet and roast them in the oven for 5 minutes. Remove them from the oven and add the pecans to a food processor. Process them until the mixture has an almost smooth consistency, creating pecan butter. Set the pecan butter aside.

FOR THE CAKE: Keep the oven at 350°F (177°C) after roasting the pecans. Spray three 6-inch (15-cm), round baking pans with baking spray.

(continued)

BUTTER PECAN CAKE WITH BROWNED BUTTER CREAM CHEESE FROSTING

(CONTINUED)

BROWNED BUTTER CREAM CHEESE FROSTING

Prepared browned butter

8 oz (226 g) cream cheese, room temperature

1 tsp vanilla extract

½ tsp salt

5 cups (600 g) confectioners' sugar

GARNISH

Chopped pecans

In a stand mixer with the paddle attachment or a large mixing bowl with a hand mixer, beat the eggs, granulated sugar and brown sugar on medium speed for 3 to 4 minutes or until the mixture is fluffy and lighter in color. Add the butter, oil, vanilla, butter pecan extract and butter extract, if using, and beat the mixture for 30 seconds. Add in the sour cream and buttermilk, and mix until everything is incorporated. Add the baking powder, baking soda and salt, and then add the flour 1 cup (125 g) at a time, scraping down the sides of the bowl as needed. After adding the last portion of flour, beat the batter just until it is combined. Mix in the prepared pecan butter.

Divide the batter into the three 6-inch (15-cm) pans. Bake for 35 to 40 minutes, or until a toothpick inserted in the center comes out clean or with a few crumbs. Allow the cake layers to cool completely on a wire rack.

FOR THE FROSTING: In a stand mixer with the paddle attachment or a large mixing bowl with a hand mixer, beat the browned butter and cream cheese on medium speed for 1 minute, until it is smooth. Mix in the vanilla and salt until incorporated. Add the confectioners' sugar 1 cup (120 g) at a time, stopping to scrape down the sides of the bowl as needed. Beat on medium speed until whipped and fluffy, about 2 to 3 minutes.

ASSEMBLY: Level each cake layer with a knife or a cake leveler. Place one layer on a cake board and frost it evenly. Add the second layer and frost. Top with the third layer. Make a crumb coat by applying a thin layer of the frosting around and on top of the cake. Refrigerate the cake for 25 to 30 minutes or until the frosting is set.

Add the remaining frosting to a pastry bag and cut about 1 inch (2.5 cm) from the tip. Going from the bottom to the top of the cake in a diagonal line, pipe large dots of buttercream. Then, smooth down half of each dot using a small spoon or spatula. Continue piping dots and smoothing them in diagonal lines all around the sides of the cake until the cake is completely covered.

Garnish the top of the cake with chopped pecans.

LEMON MERINGUE CAKE

SERVINGS: 10

Lemon meringue pie was one of my grandmother's favorite desserts. It's such a classic that she loved to make with her Sunday dinners, and I can totally see why. There's something about sweet and sour that tastes so good. Inspired by her lemon meringue pie, this cake is soft and moist with a hint of lemon and has tangy, sweet and smooth lemon curd in between each layer. Then, the whole cake is covered in silky Swiss meringue buttercream. This cake has all of the lemon filling and marshmallow meringue elements that a lemon meringue pie has. I loved her pie so much that I wanted to make it into a cake—it really is just as good in a whole new way!

LEMON CURD

4 egg yolks

⅓ cup (66 g) granulated sugar

1 tbsp (6 g) lemon zest

⅓ cup (80 ml) freshly squeezed lemon juice

1 tbsp (8 g) cornstarch

1 tbsp (15 ml) heavy cream

¼ cup + 2 tbsp (84 g) butter

CAKE

3 large eggs, room temperature

1⅓ cups (266 g) granulated sugar

¼ cup (57 g) butter, room temperature

⅔ cup (160 ml) vegetable oil

2 tsp (10 ml) vanilla extract

1 tsp lemon juice

2 tsp (4 g) lemon zest

1 cup (240 ml) sour cream, room temperature

½ cup (120 ml) buttermilk, room temperature

1 tbsp (14 g) baking powder

½ tsp baking soda

½ tsp salt

2½ cups (313 g) all-purpose flour

FOR THE LEMON CURD: In a small saucepan, place the egg yolks, sugar, lemon zest, lemon juice, cornstarch and heavy cream; whisk by hand to combine. Cook over low to medium heat, whisking constantly, until the mixture becomes thick, for 5 to 10 minutes.

Remove the curd from the heat and immediately strain it through a fine-mesh sieve over a bowl by pushing the curd through with a spoon or rubber spatula. Discard any small pieces of cooked egg left in the sieve. Add the butter and whisk until it's completely melted. Place the curd in an airtight container. Refrigerate it for 2 hours or overnight.

FOR THE CAKE: Preheat the oven to 350°F (177°C). Spray three 6-inch (15-cm), round baking pans with baking spray.

In a bowl of a stand mixer with the paddle attachment or a large mixing bowl with a hand mixer, beat the eggs and sugar on medium speed for 3 to 4 minutes, until the mixture is fluffy and lighter in color. Add the butter, oil, vanilla, lemon juice and zest, and beat the mixture for 30 seconds. Add in the sour cream and buttermilk, and mix until incorporated. Add the baking powder, baking soda and salt, then add the flour 1 cup (125 g) at a time, scraping down the sides of the bowl as needed. After adding the last portion of flour, beat the batter just until combined.

Divide the batter into the prepared cake pans. Bake for 35 to 40 minutes, until a toothpick inserted in the center comes out clean or with a few crumbs. Allow the cake layers to cool on a wire rack.

(continued)

LEMON MERINGUE CAKE

(CONTINUED)

SWISS MERINGUE BUTTERCREAM

4 egg whites

1⅓ cups (266 g) granulated sugar

1½ cups (341 g) butter, room temperature and cut into pieces

1 tsp vanilla extract

GARNISH

Dried or fresh lemon slices

Leaves

Lemon zest

FOR THE SWISS MERINGUE BUTTERCREAM: Place the egg whites and sugar into the bowl of a stand mixer or a medium heatproof bowl; whisk by hand until combined. Place the bowl over a pot with 2 to 3 inches of simmering water. Do not let the bottom of the bowl touch the water. Whisk the mixture constantly until the sugar is dissolved and the mixture has thinned out or reads 160°F (71°C) on a candy thermometer. This will take approximately 3 minutes.

Transfer the bowl to your stand mixer fitted with a whisk attachment or use the heatproof bowl with a hand mixer; whisk on medium-high for 5 to 10 minutes until the meringue is stiff and cooled.

Switch to the paddle attachment if using a stand mixer. Slowly add the softened butter 1 tablespoon (14 g) at a time and beat until smooth. Add the vanilla and beat for another 30 seconds. Place the frosting into a pastry bag, cut off about 1 inch (2.5 cm) of the tip and set aside.

ASSEMBLY: Level each cake layer with a knife or a cake leveler. Place one layer on a cake plate and pipe a ring of frosting around the outside. Fill a second piping bag with the lemon curd. Pipe the lemon curd inside the ring of frosting, enough to cover the whole area. Use an offset spatula to smooth the lemon curd. Place a second layer of cake on top. Repeat adding the frosting and lemon curd on the second layer. Place the third layer on top facedown. Make a crumb coat by applying a thin layer of the frosting around and on top of the cake. Refrigerate the cake for 25 to 30 minutes or until the frosting is set.

Pipe the frosting around the cake starting from the bottom. Pipe more frosting on top, and then use an offset spatula to smooth the top and sides. Use a large scraper to smooth the sides more until the frosting is even. Refrigerate the cake again for about 30 minutes or until set.

Place a flower petal design cake stencil around the cake. Hold the stencil in place by placing straight pins in the holes around the stencil. Use an offset spatula to add frosting to the stencil and smooth the frosting over it. Use a bench scraper to scrape off excess frosting. Remove the pins and stencil carefully. If the stencil does not cover the entire perimeter of the cake, place the stencil next to where the stenciled pattern on the cake ends. Repeat the process all the way around.

Add lemon slices and leaves to the top of the cake and then grate lemon zest on top of the garnish.

ONE-LAYER STRAWBERRY BASIL SHORTCAKE

SERVINGS: 10

When I think of summer fruit, strawberries are always the first on my list. Getting fresh, ripe strawberries at a summer's farmers market is the best! Nothing compares to those sweet berries while the weather is warm. When I was little, my mom would often make strawberry shortcakes by slicing the berries in a bowl, adding teaspoons of sugar to them and letting them sit out until the sugared strawberries created a thick syrup. Then, she would add them to those little mini pre-baked cakes you get at the supermarket and pile them high with whipped cream. Back then, it was the best! Now, I've updated the recipe by making a one-layer vanilla cake instead of those store-bought cakes, but I still use those sugared strawberries with thick whipped cream. This recipe is a summer's dream.

CAKE

3 egg whites, room temperature

¾ cup (150 g) granulated sugar

2 tbsp (28 g) butter, room temperature

¼ cup (60 ml) vegetable oil

2 tsp (10 ml) vanilla extract

1 tsp lemon juice

½ tsp lemon zest

¾ cup (180 ml) sour cream, room temperature

2 tsp (9 g) baking powder

½ tsp salt

1¼ cups (150 g) cake flour

TOPPING

1½ cups (249 g) sliced strawberries

2 tsp (8 g) granulated sugar

¼ tsp minced fresh basil

WHIPPED CREAM

1 cup (240 ml) heavy cream

2 tbsp (16 g) confectioners' sugar

½ tsp vanilla extract

FOR THE CAKE: Preheat the oven to 350°F (177°C). Spray one 8-inch (20-cm), round baking pan with baking spray.

In a stand mixer with the paddle attachment or a large mixing bowl with a hand mixer, beat the egg whites and granulated sugar on medium speed for 3 to 4 minutes, or until the mixture is fluffy. Add the butter, oil, vanilla, lemon juice and zest, and beat the mixture for about 30 seconds. Add in the sour cream, and mix until everything is incorporated. Add the baking powder, salt and cake flour, and beat the batter just until combined.

Pour the batter into the prepared cake pan. Bake for 40 to 45 minutes, until a toothpick inserted in the center comes out clean or with a few crumbs. Allow the cake to cool on a wire rack.

FOR THE TOPPING: Add the strawberries, granulated sugar and basil to a small bowl. Mix and set aside to macerate until ready to use.

FOR THE WHIPPED CREAM: Add the heavy cream, confectioners' sugar and vanilla to a medium bowl. With a hand mixer, beat the cream until it forms stiff peaks. Set this aside.

ASSEMBLY: Level the cake layer with a knife or a cake leveler. Place the cake on a cake stand. Dollop the whipped cream generously on top of the cake. Top with the macerated strawberries.

PEACHES & CREAM CAKE

SERVINGS: 10

Peaches were my grandmother's favorite fruit, so they've always been a staple in our house during the summer—we ate them cut up on top of a bowl of ice cream, in pies, or just biting right into them. So, I knew I wanted to create a cake that showcased the fruit my grandmother loved. And a peaches and cream cake sounded perfect. This cake has moist, spongy vanilla cake layers with fluffy cream cheese, whipped cream and fresh, lightly sweetened sliced peaches between each soft layer. I'm sure my grandmother would have loved it!

CAKE

3 large eggs, room temperature

1⅓ cups (266 g) granulated sugar

¼ cup (57 g) butter, room temperature

⅔ cup (160 ml) vegetable oil

2 tsp (10 ml) vanilla extract

1 tsp peach extract, optional

1 cup (240 ml) sour cream, room temperature

½ cup (120 ml) buttermilk, room temperature

1 tbsp (14 g) baking powder

½ tsp salt

2½ cups (300 g) cake flour

PEACHES

3 cups (420 g) fresh, thinly sliced peaches (3 to 4 peaches)

⅓ cup (66 g) granulated sugar

FOR THE CAKE: Preheat the oven to 350°F (177°C). Spray three 6-inch (15-cm), round baking pans with baking spray.

In a stand mixer with the paddle attachment or a large mixing bowl with a hand mixer, beat the eggs and sugar on medium speed for 3 to 4 minutes, or until the mixture is fluffy and lighter in color. Add the butter, oil, vanilla, and peach extract, if using, and beat the mixture for about 30 seconds. Add in the sour cream and buttermilk, and mix until everything is incorporated. Add the baking powder and salt, then the flour 1 cup (120 g) at a time, scraping down the sides of the bowl as needed. After adding the last portion of flour, beat the batter just until combined.

Divide the batter into three 6-inch (15-cm) pans. Bake for 35 to 40 minutes, until a toothpick inserted in the center comes out clean or with a few crumbs. Cool the cake layers on a wire rack.

FOR THE PEACHES: Add the peaches to a medium-sized bowl. Sprinkle them with the sugar and gently stir to coat the peaches with the sugar. Let the peaches sit for 25 to 30 minutes to dissolve the sugar. Keep the liquid that will be leftover from the mixture in the bowl, which we will use to soak the cake layers.

(continued)

PEACHES & CREAM CAKE

(CONTINUED)

WHIPPED CREAM FROSTING
8 oz (226 g) cream cheese, room temperature

1 cup (120 g) confectioners' sugar

1 tsp vanilla extract

2 cups (480 ml) heavy cream, cold

GARNISH
Peach slices

Flowers

FOR THE FROSTING: On medium to high speed, using a hand or a stand mixer with the whisk attachment, beat the cream cheese, confectioners' sugar and vanilla until smooth. Slowly add the heavy cream. Continue whipping until the frosting forms stiff peaks. Add the frosting to a piping bag, cut off about 1 inch (2.5 cm) of the tip, and then set it aside.

ASSEMBLY: Level each cake layer with a knife or a cake leveler. Place one layer on a cake plate. Remove about 1 tablespoon (15 ml) of the peach juice made from marinating the peaches and sugar and drizzle it on the cake layer. Pipe a swirl of whipped cream frosting on top until it covers the layer. Cover the frosting with sliced peaches. Lay the second cake layer on top of the peaches. Repeat the process. Add the third cake layer. Pipe a thin layer of the whipped cream frosting around the outside of the cake. Use a bench scraper to smooth the sides of the cake and keep some areas of cake peeking through.

Top the cake with additional whipped cream frosting, peach slices and flowers.

OLIVE OIL STONE FRUIT CAKE

SERVINGS: 10

Every summer, I look forward to stone fruit season. Peaches, plums, cherries, nectarines, apricots, pluots and some berries fit right into the stone fruit category. I love baking and cooking with them, and even just eating them plain. This cake encompasses a lot of different stone fruits. I make them into a compote that gets spread between the vanilla cake layers with a creamy layer of mascarpone cheese filling. This is the cake you want at the center of the summer entertaining table!

STONE FRUIT COMPOTE

2 medium peaches

1 small plum

1–2 apricots

3–4 cherries, optional

1 tbsp (13 g) granulated sugar, or more to taste

3 tbsp (45 ml) water, plus more if needed

1 tsp lemon juice

MASCARPONE FILLING

1 cup (232 g) mascarpone cheese, room temperature

Pinch of kosher salt

⅓ cup (40 g) confectioners' sugar

½ cup (120 ml) heavy cream

1 tsp lemon juice

FOR THE STONE FRUIT COMPOTE: Slice all of the fruit in half and remove the pits. Chop them into small pieces and add them to a small saucepan. Add the granulated sugar, water and lemon juice. Simmer over low to medium heat, stirring occasionally, for 10 minutes or until the fruit is cooked and the mixture thickens. Add more sugar to your desired taste. Add additional water by the tablespoon (15 ml) if all of the liquid cooks away. Remove the compote from the heat, cool completely and refrigerate it until ready to use.

FOR THE MASCARPONE FILLING: In a medium-sized bowl, add the mascarpone cheese, salt and confectioners' sugar. Beat with a hand mixer until the sugar is incorporated. Add the heavy cream and lemon juice. Beat again until fluffy. Refrigerate the mascarpone filling until it's ready to use.

(continued)

OLIVE OIL STONE FRUIT CAKE

(CONTINUED)

CAKE

3 large eggs, room temperature

1⅓ cups (266 g) granulated sugar

⅔ cup (160 ml) olive oil

1 tbsp (15 ml) vanilla extract

1 cup (240 ml) sour cream, room temperature

½ cup (120 ml) buttermilk, room temperature

1 tbsp (14 g) baking powder

½ tsp baking soda

½ tsp salt

2½ cups (313 g) all-purpose flour

GARNISH

Additional stone fruits

Fresh herbs

FOR THE CAKE: Preheat the oven to 350°F (177°C). Spray two 8-inch (20-cm), round baking pans with baking spray.

In a stand mixer with the paddle attachment or a large mixing bowl with a hand mixer, beat the eggs and sugar on medium speed for 3 to 4 minutes, or until the mixture is fluffy and lighter in color. Add the olive oil and vanilla and beat the mixture for 30 seconds. Add in the sour cream and buttermilk, and mix until incorporated. Add the baking powder, baking soda and salt, and then add the flour 1 cup (125 g) at a time, scraping down the sides of the bowl as needed. After adding the last portion of flour, beat the batter just until everything is combined.

Divide the batter evenly among the two pans. Bake for 40 to 45 minutes, until a toothpick inserted in the center comes out clean or with a few crumbs. Cool the cake layers completely on a wire rack.

ASSEMBLY: Level each cake layer with a knife or a cake leveler. Place one layer on a cake plate and spread about ⅓ to ½ cup (77 to 116 g) of mascarpone filling evenly on the layer. Top the filling with a layer of the stone fruit compote. Add the second cake layer and repeat with the filling and compote. Garnish the cake with more stone fruits and fresh herbs.

COCONUT CAKE WITH LIME CURD

SERVINGS: 10

Coconut cake has always been my mother's choice for her birthday cake. My grandmother made it for her every year. Now, I've taken over the baking tradition. Vanilla cake layers with a hint of coconut are paired with vanilla frosting and shredded coconut all over the outside. In this version, I've added a rich, thick coconut lime pastry cream filling. It really puts this cake over–the–top!

LIME CURD

4 egg yolks

⅓ cup (66 g) granulated sugar

1 tbsp (6 g) lime zest

⅓ cup (80 ml) freshly squeezed lime juice

1 tbsp (8 g) cornstarch

1 tbsp (15 ml) heavy cream

¼ cup + 2 tbsp (84 g) butter

Green food coloring, optional

CAKE

3 large eggs, room temperature

1⅓ cups (266 g) granulated sugar

¼ cup (57 g) butter, room temperature

⅔ cup (160 ml) vegetable oil

2 tsp (10 ml) vanilla extract

1 tsp coconut extract

1 cup (240 ml) sour cream, room temperature

½ cup (120 ml) buttermilk, room temperature

1 tbsp (14 g) baking powder

½ tsp baking soda

½ tsp salt

2½ cups (313 g) all-purpose flour

FOR THE LIME CURD: In a small saucepan, place the egg yolks, sugar, lime zest, lime juice, cornstarch and heavy cream and whisk by hand to combine. Cook the mixture over low to medium heat, whisking constantly, until it becomes thick, for 5 to 10 minutes.

Remove the curd from the heat and immediately strain it through a fine sieve over a bowl by pushing the curd through with a spoon or rubber spatula. Discard any small pieces of cooked egg left in the sieve. Add the butter and whisk until it's completely melted. Place the curd in an airtight container. Add food coloring, if using, and refrigerate the curd for 2 hours or overnight.

FOR THE CAKE: Preheat the oven to 350°F (177°C). Spray three 6-inch (15-cm), round baking pans with baking spray.

In the bowl of a stand mixer with the paddle attachment or a large mixing bowl with a hand mixer, beat the eggs and sugar on medium speed for 3 to 4 minutes, until the mixture is fluffy and lighter in color. Add the butter, oil, vanilla and coconut extracts and beat the mixture for 30 seconds. Add in the sour cream and buttermilk and mix until everything is incorporated. Add the baking powder, baking soda and salt, and then add the flour 1 cup (125 g) at a time, scraping down the sides of the bowl as needed. After adding the last portion of flour, beat the batter just until combined.

Divide the batter into the prepared cake pans. Bake for 35 to 40 minutes, until a toothpick inserted in the center comes out clean or with a few crumbs. Cool the cake layers completely on a wire rack.

(continued)

COCONUT CAKE WITH LIME CURD

(CONTINUED)

BUTTERCREAM FROSTING

1½ cups (341 g) butter, room temperature

½ tsp vanilla extract

5 cups (600 g) confectioners' sugar

3 tbsp (45 ml) heavy cream

GARNISH

Unsweetened coconut flakes or shredded coconut for the outside

Lime slices for the top

FOR THE FROSTING: In a stand mixer with the paddle attachment or a large mixing bowl with a hand mixer, beat the butter on medium speed for 1 minute, until it's smooth. Mix in the vanilla until it is incorporated. Add the confectioners' sugar 1 cup (120 g) at a time, stopping to scrape down the sides of the bowl as needed. Add the heavy cream, and then beat on medium speed until whipped and fluffy, for 2 to 3 minutes.

Add two-thirds of the frosting to a piping bag. Cut ½ inch (1.3 cm) off the tip of the bag. Add the remaining frosting to a second piping bag fitted with a star tip. Set aside both piping bags until you are ready to use them.

ASSEMBLY: Level each cake layer with a knife or cake leveler. Place one layer on a cake plate and pipe a ring of frosting around the outside. Fill a new piping bag with the lime curd. Pipe the lime curd inside the ring of frosting. Use an offset spatula to smooth it. Place a second layer of cake on top. Repeat adding the frosting and lime curd to the second layer. Place the third layer on top face down. Make a crumb coat by applying a thin layer of the frosting around and on top of the cake. Refrigerate the cake for 25 to 30 minutes or until the frosting is set.

Add the shredded coconut to the sides of the cake until all of the sides are covered. Take the bag of frosting with the star tip and pipe about six mounds of frosting around the top of the cake. Add slices of limes between the frosting mounds to finish.

CHOCOLATE CHIP COOKIE CAKE WITH COOKIE BUTTER FROSTING

Chocolate chip cookies are a classic cookie and one of my favorites! So, turning this classic cookie into a cake, I used creamy cookie butter in the batter to get that buttery cookie taste. Then, mini chocolate chips are stirred in to finish off that amazing chocolate chip cookie look and taste. Adding cookie butter to the frosting as well just makes this cake that much better.

SERVINGS: 10

CAKE

3 large eggs, room temperature

¼ cup (50 g) granulated sugar

1 cup (220 g) packed light brown sugar

¼ cup (57 g) butter, room temperature

⅔ cup (160 ml) vegetable oil

½ cup (120 g) cookie butter

1 tbsp (15 ml) vanilla extract

½ tsp butter extract, optional

1 cup (240 ml) sour cream, room temperature

½ cup (120 ml) buttermilk, room temperature

1 tbsp (14 g) baking powder

½ tsp baking soda

½ tsp salt

2½ cups (313 g) all-purpose flour

1 cup (168 g) mini chocolate chips

FOR THE CAKE: Preheat the oven to 350°F (177°C). Spray three 6-inch (15-cm), round baking pans with baking spray.

In a stand mixer with the paddle attachment or a large mixing bowl with a hand mixer, beat the eggs, granulated sugar and brown sugar on medium speed for 3 to 4 minutes, or until the mixture is fluffy and lighter in color. Add the butter, oil, cookie butter, vanilla and butter extract, if using, and beat the mixture for about 30 seconds. Add in the sour cream and buttermilk and mix until everything is incorporated. Add the baking powder, baking soda and salt, and then add the flour 1 cup (125 g) at a time, scraping down the sides of the bowl as needed. After adding the last portion of flour, beat the batter just until combined. Stir in the chocolate chips.

Divide the batter evenly among the three pans. Bake for 35 to 40 minutes, until a toothpick inserted in the center comes out clean or with a few crumbs. Cool the cake layers completely on a wire rack.

(continued)

CHOCOLATE CHIP COOKIE CAKE WITH COOKIE BUTTER FROSTING

(CONTINUED)

FROSTING
1½ cups (341 g) butter, room temperature

¾ cup (180 g) cookie butter

½ tsp vanilla extract

5 cups (600 g) confectioners' sugar

3 tbsp (45 ml) heavy cream

2–3 tbsp (10–15 g) cocoa powder

GARNISH
Eucalyptus leaves and branches, optional

FOR THE FROSTING: In a stand mixer with the paddle attachment or a large mixing bowl with a hand mixer, beat the butter and cookie butter on medium speed for 1 minute, until smooth. Mix in the vanilla until it is incorporated. Add the confectioners' sugar 1 cup (120 g) at a time, stopping to scrape down the sides of the bowl as needed. Add the heavy cream, and then beat on medium speed until whipped and fluffy, for 2 to 3 minutes.

ASSEMBLY: Level each cake layer with a knife or a cake leveler. Place one layer on a cake plate and frost it evenly. Add the second layer and frost. Top with the third layer. Make a crumb coat by applying a thin layer of the frosting around and on top of the cake. Refrigerate the cake for 25 to 30 minutes or until the frosting is set.

Divide the remaining frosting into two bowls. Add the cocoa powder, one tablespoon (5 g) at a time, to one of the bowls, until the frosting becomes a rich shade of brown.

With an offset spatula, add the lighter frosting to the top half of the cake, smoothing it all around and on top of the cake. With the same offset spatula, add the darker frosting to the bottom half of the cake, mixing the 2 colors slightly at the line where they meet. Take a large scraper to smooth the sides until the frosting is even on the cake.

Garnish the cake with leaves and branches, if desired.

COOKIES & CREAM CAKE

SERVINGS: 10

I love cookies and cream ice cream. I mean anything involving Oreos® is going to be delicious. When I was little, we'd often go for ice cream in the summer. And if I didn't get vanilla, cookies and cream was always my other choice. So, I turned one of my favorite ice cream flavors into a layer cake, and just to be over-the-top, the cake gets frosted with a dark chocolate frosting. Can a dessert get any better than this? I don't think so . . .

CAKE

6 egg whites, room temperature (180 g)

1⅓ cups (266 g) granulated sugar

¼ cup (57 g) butter, room temperature

⅔ cup (160 ml) vegetable oil

1 tbsp (15 ml) clear vanilla extract

1 cup (240 ml) sour cream, room temperature

½ cup (120 ml) buttermilk, room temperature

1 tbsp (14 g) baking powder

½ tsp baking soda

½ tsp salt

2½ cups (313 g) all-purpose flour

10–12 Oreo cookies, crushed

DARK CHOCOLATE FROSTING

1½ cups (341 g) unsalted butter

⅔ cup (66 g) Dutch processed cocoa

1 tsp vanilla extract

5 cups (600 g) confectioners' sugar

⅓ cup (80 ml) heavy cream

FOR THE CAKE: Preheat the oven to 350°F (177°C). Spray three 6-inch (15-cm), round baking pans with baking spray.

In a stand mixer with the paddle attachment or a large mixing bowl with a hand mixer, beat the egg whites and granulated sugar on medium speed for 3 to 4 minutes, or until the mixture is fluffy and lighter in color. Add the butter, oil and vanilla and beat the mixture for 30 seconds. Add in the sour cream and buttermilk and mix until incorporated. Add the baking powder, baking soda and salt, and then the flour 1 cup (125 g) at a time. After adding the last portion of flour, beat the batter just until combined. Stir in the crushed Oreos.

Divide the batter equally among the prepared pans. Bake for 35 to 40 minutes, until a toothpick inserted in the center comes out clean or with a few crumbs. Cool the cake layers completely on a wire rack.

FOR THE FROSTING: In a stand mixer with the paddle attachment or a large mixing bowl with a hand mixer, beat the butter and cocoa powder on medium speed for 1 minute, until it's smooth. Mix in the vanilla until it is incorporated. Mix in the confectioners' sugar 1 cup (120 g) at a time. Add the heavy cream, and then beat on medium speed until the frosting is fluffy, for 2 to 3 minutes.

ASSEMBLY: Level each cake layer with a knife or a cake leveler. Place one layer on a cake plate and frost it evenly. Add the second layer and frost. Top with the third layer. Make a crumb coat by applying a thin layer of the frosting around and on top of the cake. Refrigerate the cake for 25 to 30 minutes or until the frosting is set. Apply a second layer of frosting to the sides and smooth it with the scraper. Use a cake comb to create a lined pattern around the cake. Add the remaining frosting to a pastry bag fitted with a large star tip. Pipe the frosting in a tight circular motion all around the top of the cake.

CHOCOLATE MOUSSE CAKE

I just recently started loving chocolate mousse. It wasn't something that I grew up with. Since my family aren't big chocolate fans, chocolate was rarely in my house, but I definitely made up for it as an adult. Chocolate desserts are some of my favorites now, and this chocolate mousse cake makes up for the lack of chocolate I had growing up. Moist, rich chocolate layers are filled with a thick mousse and adorned with holiday chocolate pinecones. This is the cake you want for the holidays!

CAKE

2 large eggs, room temperature

2 cups (400 g) granulated sugar

½ cup (120 ml) vegetable oil

¾ cup (66 g) Dutch processed cocoa

2 tsp (10 ml) vanilla extract

1½ cups (360 ml) buttermilk, room temperature

1 tbsp (14 g) baking powder

1 tsp baking soda

1 tsp salt

2 cups (250 g) all-purpose flour

½ cup (120 ml) boiling water or coffee

CHOCOLATE MOUSSE

4 large egg yolks

¼ cup (50 g) granulated sugar

2 cups (480 ml) heavy cream, divided

3.5 oz (99 g) bittersweet chocolate bar

2 tsp (10 ml) vanilla extract

FOR THE CAKE: Preheat the oven to 350°F (177°C). Spray two 8-inch (20-cm), round baking pans with baking spray.

In the bowl of a stand mixer with the paddle attachment or a large mixing bowl with a hand mixer, beat the eggs and sugar on medium speed for 3 to 4 minutes, or until the mixture is fluffy and lighter in color. Add the oil, cocoa powder and vanilla, and beat the mixture for about 30 seconds. Add in the buttermilk and mix until it is incorporated. Add the baking powder, baking soda and salt, then add the flour 1 cup (125 g) at a time, scraping down the sides of the bowl as needed. After adding the last portion of flour, beat the batter just until combined.

Stir in the boiling water. Divide the batter equally between the two prepared pans. Bake for 40 to 45 minutes, until a toothpick inserted in the center comes out clean or with a few crumbs. Cool the cake layers completely on a wire rack.

FOR THE MOUSSE: In a medium-sized mixing bowl, whip the egg yolks and sugar with a hand mixer on high speed until fluffy, for 2 minutes. Set this aside.

Heat 1 cup (240 ml) of the heavy cream in a small saucepan over low heat, just until it starts to simmer. Do not let it boil. Remove the cream from the heat. While whisking the egg mixture, slowly pour in the warm cream mixture, a little at a time, to temper the egg yolks. Keep whisking the mixture between each pour. Then pour everything back into the saucepan.

(continued)

CHOCOLATE MOUSSE CAKE

(CONTINUED)

CHOCOLATE FROSTING

1½ cups (341 g) unsalted butter, room temperature

⅔ cup (66 g) cocoa powder

1 tsp vanilla extract

5 cups (600 g) confectioners' sugar

⅓ cup (80 ml) heavy cream

CHOCOLATE PINECONES

1½ cups (252 g) chocolate chips

⅔ cup (205 g) sweetened condensed milk

2 tbsp (28 g) unsalted butter

¼ tsp vanilla extract

¼ cup (42 g) chocolate candy melts

1½ cups (162 g) sliced almonds

¼ cup (22 g) cocoa powder

Cook over low heat, whisking constantly, until the mixture thickens slightly, for 3 to 5 minutes. Remove the mixture from the heat. Add in the chocolate and stir until fully incorporated. Place a fine-mesh strainer over a medium-sized bowl and pour in the mixture. Use a rubber spatula to press the mixture through the strainer to remove any small pieces of cooked egg. Mix in the vanilla. Let the mixture cool to room temperature, but do not let it get cold.

Meanwhile, in a medium bowl, add the remaining heavy cream and beat with a hand mixer until it forms stiff peaks. Use a rubber spatula to gently fold the whipped cream into the chocolate custard mixture. Refrigerate the mousse until ready to use.

FOR THE FROSTING: In a stand mixer with the paddle attachment or a large mixing bowl with a hand mixer, beat the butter and cocoa powder on medium speed for 1 minute, until it's smooth. Mix in the vanilla until incorporated. Add the confectioners' sugar 1 cup (120 g) at a time, stopping to scrape down the sides of the bowl as needed. Add the heavy cream, and then beat on medium speed until the frosting is whipped and fluffy, for 2 to 3 minutes. Add the frosting to a piping bag. Cut a ½ inch (1.3 cm) off the tip of the bag and set aside.

FOR THE CHOCOLATE PINECONES: Combine the chocolate chips, condensed milk, butter and vanilla in a large heatproof bowl and set it over a small pot of boiling water. Stir well until all of the chocolate and butter is melted and the mixture is smooth.

Cover the mixture with plastic wrap. Place the bowl into the refrigerator for 45 minutes to allow it to firm up enough to roll. Do not leave it in the refrigerator too long and let the mixture get too cold. It should be at room temperature and a fudge-like consistency.

Line a baking pan with parchment paper. Scoop about ¼ cup (52 g) of the pinecone mixture onto the parchment and roll it into an oval shape. Repeat to make a total of four ovals.

Add the chocolate candy melts to a microwave-safe bowl and microwave for about 50 seconds. The chocolate will not look melted after removing it from the microwave, so stir it until smooth. If still not melted after stirring, continue to microwave in 10 second bursts, stirring well after each one, until fully melted. Dip the bottom of a sliced almond in the melted candy melts and press it at the bottom of one of the oval fudge pieces, using the melted chocolate as a "glue." Dip a second sliced almond, then place it next to the first one, overlapping it a bit. Continue to add the dipped sliced almonds, working from the bottom to the top, until all of the fudge ovals are covered with almonds. Refrigerate for 30 minutes to allow them to set.

ASSEMBLY: Level each cake layer with a knife or a cake leveler. Slice each layer in half evenly, so that there are now four layers of cake. Place one layer on a cake plate and pipe a ring of frosting around the outside. Add chocolate mousse to a piping bag and cut off the bottom of the bag. Pipe the mousse inside of the frosting ring until the cake is covered. Add the second cake layer on top. Pipe another ring of chocolate frosting around the outside and fill with more of the mousse inside of the frosting ring like the first layer. Repeat with the third layer.

Add the fourth layer and make a crumb coat by applying a thin layer of the frosting around and on top of the cake. Refrigerate the cake for 25 to 30 minutes or until the frosting is set.

Pipe the remaining chocolate frosting around the sides and top of the cake. Smooth the frosting with an offset spatula until it's smooth all around. Add the chocolate pinecones to the top of the cake to decorate. Add the cocoa powder to a hand sifter and sprinkle it on top of the pinecones. Refrigerate the cake until ready to serve.

CARROT CAKE WITH ORANGE CHEESECAKE FILLING

SERVINGS: 10

Carrot cake is a dessert that we always make in the spring. It's so delicious! Carrot cake is naturally more moist than most cakes. It's the combination of the carrots and vegetable oil that does the trick. In this version, you'll find creamy orange cheesecake filling in between the layers, which makes this version of the cake even better than others. This is definitely one recipe you'll want to make again and again!

CHEESECAKE FILLING

8 oz (226 g) cream cheese

⅓ cup (104 g) sweetened condensed milk

1 tsp freshly squeezed orange juice (from zested orange)

1 tsp orange zest

CAKE

3 large eggs, room temperature

2 cups (400 g) granulated sugar

¾ cup (180 ml) vegetable oil

1 tbsp (15 ml) vanilla extract

¾ cup (180 ml) buttermilk, room temperature

2 cups (220 g) finely grated carrots

1 tbsp (14 g) baking powder

2 tsp (9 g) baking soda

½ tsp salt

2 tsp (5 g) cinnamon

¼ tsp nutmeg

2 cups (250 g) all-purpose flour

FOR THE CHEESECAKE FILLING: Add the cream cheese, condensed milk and orange juice and zest to a bowl. Beat the mixture with a hand mixer until it is smooth. Place the filling in an airtight container. Refrigerate the filling overnight for it to set.

FOR THE CAKE: Preheat the oven to 350°F (177°C). Spray three 6-inch (15-cm) pans with baking spray. Set aside.

In a stand mixer with the paddle attachment or a large mixing bowl with a hand mixer, beat the eggs and sugar on medium speed for 3 to 4 minutes, until the mixture is fluffy and lighter in color. Add the oil and vanilla and beat the mixture for 30 seconds. Add in the buttermilk and mix until it is incorporated. Mix in the grated carrots. Add the baking powder, baking soda, salt, cinnamon and nutmeg, and then add the flour 1 cup (125 g) at a time, scraping down the sides of the bowl as needed. After adding the last portion of flour, beat the batter just until combined.

Divide the batter between the baking pans. Bake for 40 to 50 minutes, until a toothpick inserted in the center comes out clean or with a few crumbs. Cool the cake layers completely on a wire rack.

(continued)

CARROT CAKE WITH ORANGE CHEESECAKE FILLING

(CONTINUED)

VANILLA FROSTING

1½ cups (341 g) butter, room temperature

1 tsp vanilla extract

5 cups (600 g) confectioners' sugar

3 tbsp (45 ml) heavy cream

GARNISH

Fresh rosemary

Eucalyptus leaves

Small berry or flowering branches

FOR THE FROSTING: In a stand mixer with the paddle attachment or a large mixing bowl with a hand mixer, beat the butter on medium speed for 1 minute, until it's smooth. Mix in the vanilla until it is incorporated. Add the confectioners' sugar 1 cup (120 g) at a time, stopping to scrape down the sides of the bowl as needed. Add the heavy cream, and then beat the frosting on medium speed for 2 to 3 minutes, until it is whipped and fluffy.

Add half of the frosting to fill a piping bag. Cut ½ inch (1.3 cm) off the tip of the bag. Add the remaining frosting to a piping bag fitted with a Wilton 127D rose petal decorating tip. Set both piping bags aside until you are ready to use them.

ASSEMBLY: Level each cake layer with a knife or cake leveler. Place one layer on a cake plate. Using the piping bag with no tip attached, pipe a ring of frosting around the outside. Fill a new piping bag with the filling and pipe half of the filling on the inside of the ring of frosting. Use an offset spatula to smooth the filling. Place a second layer of cake on top. Repeat adding the frosting and filling on the second layer. Place the third layer on top face down. Make a crumb coat by applying a thin layer of the frosting around and on top of the cake. Refrigerate the cake for 25 to 30 minutes or until the frosting is set.

Take the second piping bag with the 127D tip. Hold the tip to the bottom of the cake and pipe a straight line from the bottom to the top. Repeat with a second icing line slightly overlapping the first. Repeat until the whole cake is covered with the icing lines.

Garnish the top of the cake with fresh rosemary, leaves and branches.

BLUEBERRY, LEMON & LAVENDER SHEET CAKE

SERVINGS: 12 TO 15

Sheet cakes are one of the easiest cakes to make for a celebration. Just pour the cake batter into one pan, bake and frost. This cake is filled with a fresh jam-like lemon, blueberry and lavender compote that's swirled into the cake batter. Combining florals with desserts brings a little of nature into the recipe. The lavender is very subtle and pairs beautifully with citrus flavors and sweet-tart fruits like blueberries. Swirl some more of the flavorful jam into the frosting for a dramatic effect!

BLUEBERRY LAVENDER COMPOTE

3 cups (444 g) fresh or frozen blueberries

3 tbsp (45 g) granulated sugar

1 tbsp (15 ml) lemon juice

2 tbsp (12 g) lemon zest

2 tbsp (30 ml) water

1 tbsp (3 g) dried lavender (food-grade)

CAKE

3 large eggs, room temperature

1⅓ cups (266 g) granulated sugar

¼ cup (57 g) butter, room temperature

⅔ cup (160 ml) vegetable oil

1 tsp vanilla extract

1 tbsp (15 ml) lemon juice

1 tbsp (6 g) lemon zest

1 cup (240 ml) sour cream, room temperature

½ cup (120 ml) buttermilk, room temperature

1 tbsp (14 g) baking powder

½ tsp baking soda

½ tsp salt

2½ cups (313 g) all-purpose flour

FOR THE COMPOTE: Add the blueberries, sugar, lemon juice, lemon zest, water and lavender to a medium-sized pot over medium to high heat. Bring the mixture to a boil and use a fork or potato masher to mash the berries. Cook the mixture for 6 to 8 minutes or until the compote has reduced and thickened. Remove from the heat and set it aside to cool for use in the frosting.

FOR THE CAKE: Preheat the oven to 350°F (177°C). Spray a 9 × 13–inch (23 × 33–cm) baking pan with a small amount of cooking spray so the parchment paper will stay in place. Line the pan with two pieces of parchment paper, one going horizontal and the other vertical. Let some of the parchment hang over the sides.

In a stand mixer with the paddle attachment or a large mixing bowl with a hand mixer, beat the eggs and sugar on medium speed for 3 to 4 minutes, or until the mixture is fluffy and lighter in color. Add the butter, oil, vanilla, lemon juice and lemon zest and beat the mixture for 30 seconds. Add in the sour cream and buttermilk, and mix until everything is incorporated. Add the baking powder, baking soda and salt, and then add the flour 1 cup (125 g) at a time, scraping down the sides of the bowl as needed. After adding the last portion of flour, beat the batter just until combined.

Pour the batter into the prepared pan. With a spoon, dollop half of the compote over the batter, then use a knife to swirl it in. Bake for 40 to 45 minutes, until a toothpick inserted in the middle comes out clean or with a few crumbs. Allow the cake to cool completely.

(continued)

BLUEBERRY, LEMON & LAVENDER SHEET CAKE

(CONTINUED)

BLUEBERRY CREAM CHEESE FROSTING

½ cup (114 g) unsalted butter, room temperature

8 oz (226 g) cream cheese, room temperature

1 tsp vanilla extract

1 tsp lemon juice

2 tsp (4 g) lemon zest

3½ cups (420 g) confectioners' sugar

1–2 tbsp (15–30 ml) heavy cream

½ tsp salt

Prepared Blueberry Lavender Compote

FOR THE FROSTING: In a stand mixer with the paddle attachment or a large mixing bowl with a hand mixer, beat the butter and cream cheese on medium speed for 1 minute, until it's smooth. Mix in the vanilla, lemon juice and lemon zest until the ingredients are incorporated. Add the confectioners' sugar 1 cup (120 g) at a time, stopping to scrape down the sides of the bowl as needed. Add the heavy cream and salt, and then beat the frosting on medium speed for 2 to 3 minutes until it is whipped and fluffy.

ASSEMBLY: Add a couple of spoonfuls of the compote into the frosting and mix slightly. Spread the frosting over the cake. Add more spoonfuls of the compote on top of the frosting. Use a butter knife to swirl the compote into the frosting.

RED VELVET BUNDT CAKE

SERVINGS: 10

Red velvet cake is a southern classic and in recent years, it's been making its way all around the country. The cake has a vanilla base with a touch of cocoa. It gets its bright color from red food coloring. The recipe gets a spoonful of vinegar in it, which is used to leaven the cake, but you can't taste it. Truthfully, I had never tried red velvet cake until I was an adult, but once I did, I was forever smitten. And with this white chocolate cream cheese glaze that goes on top, you will be too!

RED VELVET CAKE

2 large eggs, room temperature

2 cups (400 g) granulated sugar

1 cup (240 ml) vegetable oil

1 tsp vanilla extract

¼ cup (60 ml) liquid red food coloring

1 cup (240 ml) buttermilk, room temperature

1 tbsp (5 g) unsweetened cocoa powder

1 tsp salt

2½ cups (313 g) all-purpose flour

1 tbsp (15 ml) vinegar

1 tsp baking soda

CREAM CHEESE GLAZE

½ cup (120 g) high-quality white chocolate chips

8 oz (226 g) cream cheese, room temperature

4 cups (480 g) confectioners' sugar

2 tbsp (30 ml) heavy cream

FOR THE CAKE: Preheat the oven to 350°F (177°C). Spray a 12-cup (2.9-L) Bundt pan with baking spray.

In a stand mixer with the paddle attachment or a large mixing bowl with a hand mixer, beat the eggs and granulated sugar on medium speed for 3 to 4 minutes, or until the mixture is fluffy and lighter in color. Add the oil, vanilla and red food coloring and beat the mixture for about 30 seconds. Add in the buttermilk and mix until incorporated. Add the cocoa powder and salt, and then add the flour 1 cup (125 g) at a time, scraping down the sides of the bowl as needed. After adding the last portion of flour, beat the batter just until combined.

Add the vinegar and baking soda to a small dish. Stir and pour the mixture into the cake batter. Mix until well incorporated. Pour the batter into the prepared Bundt pan.

Bake for 40 to 45 minutes, until a toothpick inserted in the deepest part comes out clean or with a few crumbs. Cool completely on a wire rack.

FOR THE CREAM CHEESE GLAZE: Place the white chocolate chips in a microwave-safe bowl and microwave on medium-high for 30 seconds. Stir. Continue to heat in 10-second increments, stirring each time, until all the chips are completely melted and the white chocolate is smooth.

Beat the cream cheese in a stand mixer with the paddle attachment or in a bowl with a hand mixer until smooth. Add the melted white chocolate and beat for 30 seconds more. Add in the confectioners' sugar and heavy cream. Beat the mixture until it is smooth. Drizzle the glaze over the top of the Bundt cake.

EGGNOG RUM BUNDT CAKE

SERVINGS: 10

Eggnog: You either love it or hate it. I'm definitely on the "love it" side. If it's Thanksgiving or Christmas in my house, you will always find a bottle of eggnog; I enjoy it spiked with rum with a sprinkle of nutmeg on top. It wouldn't be the holidays without it. So, turning this holiday favorite into a cake was no-brainer.

BUNDT CAKE

3 large eggs, room temperature

1¼ cups (250 g) granulated sugar

⅔ cup (160 ml) vegetable oil

1 tbsp (15 ml) vanilla extract

½ tsp cinnamon

¾ tsp nutmeg

½ cup (120 ml) sour cream, room temperature

1 cup (240 ml) eggnog, room temperature

2 tbsp (30 ml) rum

2 tsp (9 g) baking powder

½ tsp baking soda

½ tsp salt

2½ cups (300 g) cake flour

GLAZE

2 cups (240 g) confectioners' sugar

½ tsp nutmeg

½ tsp vanilla extract

¼ cup (60 ml) eggnog

2 tbsp (30 ml) rum

GARNISH

Cinnamon sticks

Rosemary sprigs

FOR THE CAKE: Preheat the oven to 350°F (177°C). Spray a 12-cup (2.9 L) Bundt pan with baking spray.

In a stand mixer with the paddle attachment or a large mixing bowl with a hand mixer, beat the eggs and granulated sugar on medium speed for 3 to 4 minutes, or until the mixture is fluffy and lighter in color. Add the oil, vanilla, cinnamon and nutmeg, and beat the mixture for 30 seconds. Add in the sour cream, eggnog and rum, and mix until all the ingredients are incorporated. Add the baking powder, baking soda and salt, and then add the flour 1 cup (120 g) at a time, scraping down the sides of the bowl as needed. After adding the last portion of flour, beat the batter just until combined.

Pour the batter into the prepared Bundt pan. Bake for 1 hour to 1 hour and 15 minutes, until a toothpick inserted in the deepest part comes out clean or with a few crumbs. Cool the cake completely on a wire rack.

FOR THE GLAZE: In a bowl, combine the confectioners' sugar, nutmeg, vanilla and eggnog. Beat with a hand mixer until smooth. Mix in the rum.

Place the cake on a cake plate and drizzle it with the glaze. Arrange the cinnamon sticks and rosemary sprigs around the cake plate for garnish.

CHOCOLATE, ESPRESSO & KAHLUA BUNDT CAKE WITH KAHLUA GLAZE

SERVINGS: 10

There seems to be a natural attraction of sweet, smooth chocolate and warm, aromatic coffee, which makes them an amazing pair! Look at all of the different types of drinks with this luscious combination like lattes, iced mochas, coffee, hot cocoa, mocha Frappuccinos and more! This chocolate Bundt cake is made with dark cocoa and strong espresso and is covered with a creamy coffee liqueur glaze.

BUNDT CAKE

2 large eggs, room temperature

2 cups (400 g) granulated sugar

½ cup (120 ml) vegetable oil

¾ cup (66 g) Dutch processed cocoa

2 tsp (10 ml) vanilla extract

1 cup (240 ml) buttermilk, room temperature

½ cup (120 ml) Kahlua

1 tbsp (14 g) baking powder

1 tsp baking soda

1 tsp salt

2 cups (250 g) all-purpose flour

½ cup (120 ml) hot espresso

KAHLUA GLAZE

1 cup (120 g) confectioners' sugar

3–4 tbsp (45–60 g) Kahlua

FOR THE CAKE: Preheat the oven to 350°F (177°C). Spray a 12-cup (2.9-L) Bundt pan with baking spray.

In a stand mixer with the paddle attachment or a large mixing bowl with a hand mixer, beat the eggs and granulated sugar on medium speed for 3 to 4 minutes, or until the mixture is fluffy and lighter in color. Add the oil, cocoa powder and vanilla, and beat the mixture for about 30 seconds. Add in the buttermilk and Kahlua, and mix until all ingredients are incorporated. Add in the baking powder, baking soda and salt, and then add the flour 1 cup (125 g) at a time, scraping down the sides of the bowl as needed. After adding the last portion of flour, beat the batter just until combined.

Stir in the espresso. Pour the batter in the prepared Bundt pan. Bake for 40 to 45 minutes, or until a toothpick inserted in the deepest part comes out clean or with a few crumbs. Cool the cake completely on a wire rack.

FOR THE KAHLUA GLAZE: Add the confectioners' sugar and Kahlua to a small mixing bowl. Beat with a hand mixer until the Kahlua and confectioners' sugar are fully incorporated. Drizzle the glaze over the cake and serve.

CREATIVE PIES FOR EVERY SEASON

GROWING UP, PIE WAS A DESSERT THAT WE HAD FOR EACH AND EVERY HOLIDAY—Thanksgiving, Christmas, Easter, you name it—and the star of the table was always my grandmother's peach cobbler, which she was famous for in the family. Even if she wasn't hosting the meal, she was expected to have that pie on the table. I often helped her when she was in the kitchen: rolling the dough, adding the sugar and spices to the sliced peaches, and then crimping the top crust. I swear, it was the best peach cobbler ever! Pie is definitely one of my favorite desserts. I'll usually choose it before anything else.

There are so many different types of pie with endless variations of crusts and fillings. You really can't go wrong with the flavor and texture combinations. In this chapter, I touch on a variety of recipes for pies, cobbler, tarts and more with fruit, custard and nut fillings. All of these pies are perfect for holidays and celebrations, because what's a celebration without pie? It's the comfort food of dessert.

There is the traditional apple pie with the addition of caramel (page 57), which is a favorite, and the not-so-traditional Pink Grapefruit Curd Tartlets (page 67). There are also the small Bourbon, Brown Sugar & Peach Hand Pies (page 62) and the large Mixed Berry Star Crust Slab Pie (page 78). Of course I had to include my grandmother's beloved Southern Peach Cobbler (page 55), which you won't want to miss trying. Each of these are a little slice of heaven, so let's dig right in!

TIP: If you want to make a pie ahead of time, put the whole pie together if it's a double crust pie. Freeze the pie for 1 hour, uncovered. Then, wrap the pie completely with plastic wrap. Then, wrap it a second time. Place it back in the freezer for up to 3 months. If it's a single crust pie, freeze the pie pan for an hour, and then wrap the crust twice. Add the filling to a ziplock plastic bag and place it on top of the pie crust. Place it in the freezer for up to 3 months.

SOUTHERN PEACH COBBLER

SERVINGS: 12

There are more ways than you might know to make the topping for peach cobbler. You can make a biscuit-like dough and drop spoonfuls on top of the peaches. You can also make a thin batter and pour that on the peaches. My grandmother always made it with pie crust on the bottom and top. Some would say, "Since there's pie crust, isn't this just a peach pie?" Well, yes, it looks like a peach pie, but we call it peach cobbler. Unlike a traditional pie, you do not cut it into slices when serving; instead, you use a large serving spoon and scoop the cobbler out of the dish. This is the way that many people make it, including my grandmother, and peach cobbler was definitely her specialty. I added my own touch to this recipe by adding a little ground cinnamon to the dough. That extra bit of spice makes the recipe that much better. Add one big scoop of creamy vanilla ice cream on top of that warm scoop of juicy peach cobbler, and it's just to die for!

CINNAMON COBBLER CRUST

5 cups (625 g) all-purpose flour

¼ cup (50 g) granulated sugar

1 tbsp (8 g) cinnamon

2 tsp (12 g) salt

2 cups (456 g) unsalted butter, cubed and frozen (European-style butter, see Note on the next page)

1½ cups (360 ml) sour cream

FILLING

6–7 cups (840–980 g) fresh peaches, peeled, pitted and sliced

1½ cups (300 g) granulated sugar

1 tsp cinnamon

½ tsp nutmeg

1 tsp lemon juice

1 tsp vanilla extract

2 tbsp (16 g) cornstarch

FOR THE CINNAMON COBBLER CRUST: Combine the flour, sugar, cinnamon and salt in a food processor. Pulse the food processor to combine all the ingredients. Add the butter and pulse for a few seconds to just combine the flour and fat. Add the sour cream and pulse again until the dough comes together. Divide the dough in half and shape each half into a disk. Wrap one disk in plastic wrap until ready to use.

On a lightly floured work surface, roll out the second disk to approximately 16 × 20 inches (41 × 51 cm). Place the rolled dough in an 8 × 13–inch (20 × 33–cm) oval or 9 × 13–inch (23 × 33–cm) rectangle baking dish. Set the crusts in the refrigerator until ready to use.

FOR THE FILLING: In a large mixing bowl, add the peaches, sugar, cinnamon, nutmeg, lemon juice, vanilla and cornstarch (if using frozen peaches, use 3 tablespoons [24 g] of flour). Mix well, and then pour the fruit into the baking dish with the rolled dough.

(continued)

SOUTHERN PEACH COBBLER

(CONTINUED)

EGG WASH
1 large egg
1 tsp milk or water

TO SERVE
Vanilla ice cream, optional

ASSEMBLY: Roll out the second disk on a lightly floured work surface slightly larger than the circumference of the pie dish. Cut even, wide strips of dough to make a lattice design. Place six to seven strips on top of the peach filling. Fold back every second strip of pastry onto itself, a bit more than halfway across the top.

Gather the excess dough and possibly some of the remaining dough, knead it into a ball, and roll the dough out again. Cut the dough into even strips. Weave the second set of strips into the first by placing a strip of pastry perpendicular to the remaining strips on the cobbler. Unfold the folded strips of pastry across the perpendicular strip of pastry. Next, fold back the other strips of pastry. Place another strip of pastry perpendicular to the original strips of pastry. Repeat this pattern with the remaining strips of pastry. Cut off the excess dough around the dish. Set the dish aside.

Sprinkle your work surface with additional flour and roll out the remaining dough. Use leaf- and flower-shaped cookie plungers and cutters to cut out differently shaped leaves and flowers. Make the egg wash by beating the egg with milk or water in a small dish. Use a pastry brush to brush the egg wash over the surface of the dough. Arrange the leaf and flower cutouts in a top corner or around the edges. Brush the egg wash over the cutouts.

Place the cobbler into the freezer for at least 30 minutes. This will help the dough cutouts hold their shape during the baking process.

Preheat the oven to 375°F (191°C). Tent the areas of the cobbler with the dough leaf and flower cutouts with foil so they do not burn. Bake for 40 minutes. Remove the foil and bake for an additional 20 to 25 minutes or until the crust is evenly browned and the filling is bubbling.

Allow the pie to cool for about an hour. Scoop large spoonful into bowls and serve with vanilla ice cream, if desired.

NOTE: European butter has a high fat content which is great for pie dough. It contains more fat and less water than regular butter, so it melts faster and makes the crust flakier. I use Kerrygold Pure Irish Unsalted Butter.

SALTED CARAMEL APPLE PIE

SERVINGS: 8

Apple pie is such a classic. And it's honestly one of my favorite pies. I probably make it for every holiday regardless of the season. Yes, I'm one of those people who bakes apple pie in the middle of the summer, even on the hottest day. This cinnamon-spiced apple pie with rich salted caramel in a homemade buttery sour cream pie crust is the perfect pie!

SALTED CARAMEL

1 cup (100 g) granulated sugar
1 cup (240 ml) heavy cream
½ cup (114 g) unsalted butter
1 tsp salt

FILLING

4–5 apples, peeled, cored and sliced
½ cup (100 g) granulated sugar
1 tsp lemon juice
2 tsp (5 g) cinnamon
1 tsp nutmeg
2 tsp (10 ml) vanilla extract
2 tbsp (16 g) all-purpose flour
½ cup (136 g) prepared salted caramel

PIE CRUST

1 recipe for the double crust Sour Cream Pie Dough (page 82)
1 egg + 1 tsp milk or water for egg wash
½ cup (50 g) turbinado sugar

FOR THE SALTED CARAMEL: In a saucepan, place the sugar over medium heat. Let the sugar melt completely. Stir the sugar slowly with a wooden spoon as it melts and turns amber in color. When all of the sugar is dissolved, slowly add the heavy cream. Be careful because the mixture will quickly bubble up. Vigorously whisk, and then add the butter, one tablespoon (14 g) at a time. When the butter is melted, turn off the heat, add the salt, and then set aside to let it cool.

FOR THE FILLING: To a bowl, add the sliced apples, sugar, lemon juice, cinnamon, nutmeg and vanilla. Mix until all the ingredients are combined. Add the flour and stir. Set aside.

ASSEMBLY: On a lightly floured work surface, roll out one pie dough disk slightly larger than the dish that will be used for the pie. Place the pie crust into a 9-inch (23-cm) pie dish. Add the filling to the pie dough. Drizzle ½ cup (136 g) of the salted caramel over the apple filling. Place the dish into the refrigerator while the top crust is rolled out.

Roll out the second half of the pie dough slightly larger than the pie dish. Cut the dough into five to seven even strips. Place the strips down on top of the apples. If no more strips remain, gather the scraps from all of the excess dough, knead the dough into a ball and roll it out. Cut the dough into strips. Weave the second set of strips into the first by placing a strip of pastry perpendicular to the remaining strips on the pie. Unfold the folded strips of pastry across the perpendicular strip of pastry. Next, fold back the other strips of pastry. Place another strip of pastry perpendicular to the original strips of pastry. Repeat this pattern with the remaining strips of pastry. Cut off the excess pie dough around the pie dish. Set aside.

(continued)

SALTED CARAMEL APPLE PIE

(CONTINUED)

Place the whole pie in the refrigerator for 30 minutes and preheat the oven to 375°F (191°C). When the oven reaches temperature, remove the pie from the refrigerator and brush the entire pie with the egg wash until all of the dough is covered. Sprinkle the turbinado sugar evenly over the pie dough.

Bake for about 1 hour or until it is browned all over. If the edges begin to brown too much, tent it with foil. Cool the pie on a wire rack.

APRICOT BLUEBERRY GALETTE

SERVINGS: 8

I think one of the prettiest tarts are galettes. Because galettes have one pastry dough on the bottom that's wrapped over and around a filling, the center of the tart is exposed and all of the filling is shown. You can leave the border the way it is crimped over the filling, or you can add dough cutouts, turbinado sugar, nuts or any other decorative accent. For this galette, fresh apricots and blueberries pair so well together thanks to their sweet and tart flavors, and adding a sprinkling of turbinado sugar to the outside of the crust makes this one beautiful galette!

FILLING

6–8 apricots, pitted and halved, skin on

⅔ cup (132 g) granulated sugar

1 tsp lemon juice

1 tsp lemon zest

1 tsp vanilla extract

2 tsp (5 g) cornstarch

1 cup (148 g) fresh blueberries

1 recipe for the single crust Cream Cheese Pie Dough (page 84)

1 large egg + 1 tsp milk or water for egg wash

¼ cup (52 g) turbinado sugar

¼ cup (80 g) apricot jam

1 tbsp (15 ml) water

Preheat the oven to 375°F (191°C).

Add the apricot halves, granulated sugar, lemon juice, lemon zest, vanilla and cornstarch to a large mixing bowl. Gently stir until all the ingredients are incorporated. Add the blueberries and lightly mix again. Set aside.

Roll out the pie dough on a parchment-lined baking surface dusted lightly with flour. Add the fruit to the center of the dough. Fold about 1 inch (2.5 cm) of the edges in over the fruit all around the perimeter of the galette. Transfer the galette with the parchment paper onto a flat, edgeless baking sheet.

Combine the egg and milk or water in a small dish. Brush the egg wash over the perimeter of the crust. Sprinkle with turbinado sugar.

Bake for 40 to 50 minutes or until the crust is browned. Melt the apricot jam and water in a small saucepan. Brush the mixture onto the fruit and serve warm.

BOURBON, BROWN SUGAR & PEACH HAND PIES

Hand pies are so cute and the perfect size. My very first recollection of a hand pie was those little fried pies from McDonalds that I had as a kid, and I'm not ashamed to say that I loved them. My palate has definitely evolved since then, and I appreciate a lovely home-made pie crust and fresh filling. Adding a splash of bourbon to these brown sugar spiced peaches is just what these hand pies need.

SERVINGS: 8 TO 10 HAND PIES

FILLING
4 peaches, peeled and cubed
3 tbsp (42 g) brown sugar
2 tbsp (30 ml) bourbon
½ tsp vanilla extract
½ tsp of cinnamon
¼ tsp nutmeg
1 tbsp (8 g) cornstarch

PIE CRUST
1 recipe for the double crust Cream Cheese Pie Dough (page 84)
1 egg + 1 tsp milk or water for egg wash

TO SERVE
Ice cream, optional

FOR THE FILLING: In a medium saucepan, add the peaches, brown sugar, bourbon, vanilla, cinnamon, nutmeg and cornstarch. Cook over medium heat until the peaches are tender and the juice has thickened. Mash the mixture with a potato masher. Remove the filling from the heat and cool completely.

ASSEMBLY: Roll out one pie dough disk on a lightly floured work surface. Use a 3-inch (8-cm), round cookie cutter and cut out eight to ten circles. Gather the scraps up in a ball and set them aside. Roll out the second dough. Cut another eight to ten circles. Gather all of the scraps together and knead them into a ball. Roll out the extra dough and use leaf and flower cookie plungers to cut out leaf and flower shapes. Also cut out strips to make braids and lattices. Place the decor on a small parchment-lined baking sheet and refrigerate until you are ready to use them.

Line a large baking pan with parchment paper. Place down half of the cutout circles. Add a tablespoon (15 ml) of the filling in the middle of each. Brush water around the perimeter of each round. Place a second circle on top of some of the hand pies. Use some of the strips to make lattices on others, and add a braid around the edges of one or two. Use a fork to crimp the edges of the hand pies.

Beat the egg and milk or water in a small dish. Brush the egg wash on top of each hand pie. Add the flowers to the top of some pies, and braids to others. Brush them with the egg wash. Place the baking sheet into the freezer for at least 30 minutes. This will help the dough cutouts hold their shape during the baking process.

Preheat the oven to 400°F (204°C). Bake for 15 to 20 minutes or until the crust browns. Remove the hand pies and let them cool slightly. Serve with ice cream, if desired.

BROWNED BUTTER SWEET POTATO PIE

SERVINGS: 8

Growing up, the one pie we always had at Thanksgiving was my great aunt's sweet potato pie, and Aunt Gladys made the absolute BEST sweet potato pie. There was not too much sugar, not too much cinnamon—it was just perfect. In the South, sweet potato pie has always been a favorite dessert in African American homes. So, when my aunt moved from Florida to New York, southern dessert recipes like sweet potato pie came with her. I don't think I even tasted a pumpkin pie until I was an adult. So, when I think of Thanksgiving, I think of sweet potato pie first. This pie recipe is just like my aunt's recipe, but with browned butter instead of regular melted butter. Browned butter gives the pie a toasty, nutty flavor that is irresistible! This recipe is for a thicker deep-dish sweet potato pie. If your pie pan is shallow, use half of the filling and freeze and save the rest for another time.

FILLING

2 cups (268 g) plain mashed sweet potatoes (2 baked sweet potatoes)

¼ cup (57 g) butter

¾ cup (165 g) packed light brown sugar

⅓ cup (66 g) granulated sugar

½ tsp cinnamon

½ tsp nutmeg

¼ tsp salt

1¼ cups (320 ml) evaporated milk

3 large eggs

1 tbsp (15 ml) vanilla extract

FOR THE FILLING: Preheat the oven to 450°F (232°C) degrees. With a fork, poke holes in the sweet potatoes, and bake them on a foil-lined baking sheet for 1 hour or until they are soft when poked. Allow them to cool completely, and then mash the potatoes.

Add the butter to a small saucepan. Melt the butter over medium heat, stirring occasionally. After it's melted, the butter will start to foam and the milk solids will turn brown. After about 5 to 7 minutes, the butter will begin to brown. When the butter is completely browned, remove it from heat, and pour it into a small heatproof bowl. Set this aside.

In a pot, place the brown sugar, granulated sugar, cinnamon, nutmeg, salt and evaporated milk. Heat until the sugar is melted. Pour the mixture into a food processor. Add the mashed sweet potatoes and the browned butter. Purée the mixture for a few seconds. Add the eggs and vanilla. Purée again until the mixture is smooth and no chunks of sweet potato remain.

(continued)

BROWNED BUTTER SWEET POTATO PIE

(CONTINUED)

PIE CRUST

1 recipe for the double crust
Sour Cream Pie Dough
(page 82) or the All Butter Pie
Dough (page 85)

1 egg + 1 tsp milk or water for
egg wash

ASSEMBLY: Preheat the oven to 350°F (177°C). Roll out one pie dough disk on a lightly floured work surface, slightly larger than the pie dish. Place the rolled dough in a deep-dish, 9-inch (23-cm) pie pan. Trim and tuck under the excess pie dough. Crimp the edges with your fingers around the perimeter of the dish. Mix the egg with 1 teaspoon of milk. Brush the egg wash along the perimeter of the pie crust.

Roll out the second disk of dough. Use cookie cutters/plungers and cut out several leaves. Lay the leaves on a parchment-lined baking sheet. Brush the remaining egg wash over the leaves. Bake the leaves for 20 minutes, or until they are browned. Set aside to cool.

Pour the sweet potato mixture inside the crust. Bake the pie for 50 to 55 minutes or until the center no longer jiggles when the pie is moved. Cool and decorate the perimeter of the pie with the crust leaves.

PINK GRAPEFRUIT CURD TARTLETS

SERVINGS: 6

Grapefruits are such a great citrus fruit. I guess I've loved eating them since the womb. My mother often tells the story of how she couldn't get enough of grapefruits when she was pregnant with me. Maybe it was me that was requesting them every day! Either way, I love them, and so I had to make tartlets with them. Rich, smooth pink grapefruit curd fills a buttery shortbread crust with a wave of toasted marshmallow meringue on top. It's such a delicious and pretty dessert!

SHORTBREAD CRUST

½ cup (114 g) unsalted butter, room temperature

¼ cup (50 g) granulated sugar

¼ tsp vanilla extract

1 cup (125 g) all-purpose flour

GRAPEFRUIT CURD

¼ cup (32 g) cornstarch

1¼ cups (250 g) granulated sugar

5 large egg yolks

1½ cups (360 ml) freshly squeezed pink grapefruit juice

½ cup (120 ml) water

1 tbsp (6 g) grapefruit zest

¼ cup (57 g) unsalted butter

FOR THE SHORTBREAD CRUST: In a stand mixer or mixing bowl with a hand mixer, add the butter and sugar. Cream until smooth. Mix in the vanilla. Add the flour and mix until all the ingredients are incorporated. Refrigerate the dough for 30 to 40 minutes.

Preheat the oven to 300°F (149°C). Divide and press the dough into six 4-inch (10-cm) tart pans with removable bottoms. Place the pans on a baking sheet and bake for 10 to 15 minutes or until they are lightly golden. Allow them to cool completely.

FOR THE GRAPEFRUIT CURD: Add the cornstarch and sugar to a medium saucepan. Add the egg yolks, grapefruit juice and water and whisk together. Place the saucepan over medium-low heat and cook, stirring often, until it gets thick and starts to bubble. This should take 8 minutes.

Remove the curd from the heat and pour it through a fine-mesh strainer into a bowl, using a spatula to push it through to remove any bits of egg. Whisk in the grapefruit zest and butter until everything is fully combined.

Spoon the grapefruit filling into the prepared tart pans and smooth over the top. Cover the baking sheet pan with plastic wrap and chill it in the refrigerator for at least 3 hours or overnight.

(continued)

PINK GRAPEFRUIT CURD TARTLETS

(CONTINUED)

MERINGUE
5 large egg whites
½ cup (100 g) granulated sugar
1 tsp cream of tartar
1 tsp vanilla extract

GARNISH
Grapefruit zest

FOR THE MERINGUE: Add the egg whites, sugar, and cream of tartar to the bowl of a stand mixer. Whisk together until everything is fully combined.

Fill a small pot with about 2 inches (5 cm) of water over medium-high heat and bring to a simmer. Set the bowl of the stand mixer over the pot of simmering water. Constantly whisk the mixture for 3 to 5 minutes, until the egg whites reach a temperature of 160°F (71°C) and all the sugar has dissolved.

Remove the bowl from the heat and attach the bowl to a stand mixer fitted with a whisk attachment. Turn the mixer on and gradually increase the speed until it reaches medium-high. You can also do this step with a hand mixer. Add in the vanilla and whip the meringue for 8 minutes, until it is glossy, begins to thicken and forms stiff peaks.

Add the meringue to a pastry bag with a St. Honore pastry tip. Remove the tarts from the pans. Make a wave pattern of meringue on top of the tartlets. Use a hand torch to lightly toast the meringue. Grate the grapefruit zest over the top and serve.

ORANGE, BOURBON & PECAN PIE

SERVINGS: 8

Pecan Pie is a classic southern dessert, and almost always graces our Thanksgiving tables. I've added a twist to this delicious favorite with Kentucky bourbon and orange zest! These combined with sugar, corn syrup, eggs and vanilla give the pie a sweet custard-like interior. The pecan-crusted top is crisp to perfection. And to make this Orange, Bourbon & Pecan Pie complete, top it with a rich, creamy bourbon whipped cream! No Thanksgiving would be complete without this delicious dessert!

PIE CRUST

1 recipe for the single crust Sour Cream Pie Dough (page 82) or All Butter Pie Dough (page 85)

1 large egg + 1 tsp milk or water for egg wash

FILLING

3 large eggs

⅔ cup (160 ml) dark corn syrup

1 cup (200 g) granulated sugar

1 tsp vanilla extract

1 tbsp (6 g) orange zest

¼ tsp salt

2 tbsp (30 ml) bourbon

⅓ cup (80 ml) melted butter

2–2½ cups (218–272 g) pecan halves

BOURBON WHIPPED CREAM

½ cup (120 ml) heavy cream

2 tsp (5 g) confectioners' sugar

½ tsp vanilla extract

1 tsp bourbon

Preheat the oven to 350°F (177°C).

FOR THE PIE CRUST: On a lightly floured work surface, roll out the pie dough and place it in the bottom of a 9-inch (23-cm) pie pan. Cut off the excess dough around the edges. You can use some of the excess dough to cut out leaf shapes to add around the outside of the pie shell.

Mix the egg with 1 teaspoon of milk in a small bowl. Brush the egg wash along the perimeter of the pie crust.

FOR THE FILLING: In a bowl, add the eggs, corn syrup, granulated sugar, vanilla, orange zest, salt, bourbon and melted butter. Mix well until all the ingredients are incorporated.

ASSEMBLY: Pour the filling into the prepared pie pan. Arrange the pecans in a single layer over the top of the filling. Bake for 45 minutes. Then, allow the pie to cool on a wire rack.

FOR THE BOURBON WHIPPED CREAM: Whisk the heavy cream in a stand mixer or in a bowl with a hand mixer until it starts to thicken. Then, add the confectioners' sugar and continue to beat it until it's thickened. Add the vanilla and bourbon and fold in until incorporated.

Serve the pie with the bourbon whipped cream.

KEY LIME TART

Every summer when I go to Florida to visit my family, the one dessert I always order at restaurants is the key lime pie. It's so good! The tartness of the limes, the sweetness of the condensed milk and that graham cracker crust is the best combo. This Key Lime Tart is a spin on the classic key lime pie. The ratio of graham cracker crust to filling is more even with this tart, as opposed to the filling being a lot thicker in the classic pie. There's also a bit of crushed walnuts in the crust which gives it a little nutty flavor. If you love key lime desserts, this is the one you need to try next!

CRUST

2 cups (168 g) graham crackers, finely crushed

¼ cup (29 g) ground walnuts (ground in a food processor)

1 tbsp (15 g) granulated sugar

6–7 tbsp (84–98 g) unsalted butter, melted

FILLING

4 large egg yolks

1 (14-oz [396-g]) can sweetened condensed milk

½ cup (120 ml) key lime juice or lime juice

2 tsp (4 g) lime zest

WHIPPED CREAM

1 cup (240 ml) cold heavy cream

2 tbsp (16 g) confectioners' sugar

1 tsp vanilla extract

GARNISH

Lime zest and slices

FOR THE CRUST: Preheat the oven to 350°F (177°C). In a medium-sized mixing bowl, mix together the crushed graham cracker crumbs, ground walnuts, granulated sugar and butter. Press the mixture firmly into the bottom and sides of a 9-inch (23-cm) tart pan. Bake for 10 to 15 minutes, and then allow it to cool completely.

FOR THE FILLING: In a stand mixer with a paddle attachment or a large bowl with a hand mixer, beat the egg yolks until they are thick and turn to a light yellow. While mixing on a low speed, slowly add the condensed milk. Gradually add the key lime juice and zest and continue to mix on a low speed just until all the ingredients are blended. Pour the mixture into the tart pan and bake for 15 minutes. Remove the tart from the oven and allow it to cool to room temperature. Refrigerate for at least 4 hours or overnight.

FOR THE WHIPPED CREAM: In a medium bowl with a hand mixer, add the heavy cream, confectioners' sugar and vanilla. Whip the cream until it forms stiff peaks.

Top the pie with the whipped cream and garnish with the lime zest and slices.

NOTE: ¼ cup (21 g) additional graham cracker crumbs can be substituted for the ground walnuts, if needed.

BLUEBERRY LEMON CRUMB PIE

SERVINGS: 8

I never really ate or made blueberry pie until after I had a blueberry crumb pie at New York City's Big Apple BBQ 12 years ago. That year, it was one of the only desserts offered at that giant barbecue feast, so I got it, reluctantly. After I took that first bite, I wondered why the heck I didn't give blueberry pie a chance sooner. It was so good. I ate it as my husband and I walked back to our car, which was probably a mistake because my concentration was definitely on that pie, so I almost ran into a couple of poles. For this blueberry pie, I added a hint of fresh lemon and topped it with a beautiful crumb topping. My one piece of advice is just to not eat it as you're walking!

FILLING

4–5 cups (592–740 g) blueberries

1 cup (200 g) granulated sugar

2 tbsp (30 ml) fresh lemon juice

1 tbsp (6 g) lemon zest

¼ tsp salt

½ tsp cinnamon

¼ tsp nutmeg

2 tbsp (16 g) cornstarch

CRUMB TOPPING

¾ cup (165 g) light brown sugar

1 cup (125 g) all-purpose flour

½ tsp cinnamon

¼ cup (57 g) butter

PIE CRUST

1 recipe for the single crust Sour Cream Pie Dough (page 82) or All Butter Pie Dough (page 85)

1 large egg + 1 tsp milk or water for egg wash

Preheat the oven to 375°F (191°C).

FOR THE FILLING: In a large mixing bowl, add the blueberries, granulated sugar, lemon juice, lemon zest, salt, cinnamon, nutmeg and cornstarch. Mix well until all the ingredients are incorporated. Set aside.

FOR THE CRUMB TOPPING: Add the brown sugar, flour and cinnamon to a medium-sized mixing bowl. Add the butter and cut it into the flour and sugar mixture by using a fork, a pastry cutter or your fingers. Place the bowl into the refrigerator until ready to use.

FOR THE PIE CRUST: Roll out one pie dough disk on a lightly floured work surface, slightly larger than the pie dish. Place the dough in a 9-inch (23-cm) pie dish. Trim and tuck under the excess pie dough. Crimp the edges with your fingers around the perimeter of the dish.

Mix the egg with 1 teaspoon of milk or water in a small bowl. Brush the egg wash along the perimeter of the pie crust.

ASSEMBLY: Pour the filling into the pie dish. Sprinkle the crumble on top and spread it out over the filling. Place the pie into the freezer for at least 30 minutes.

Place the pie on a parchment-lined baking sheet and bake for 45 minutes to an hour, or until the crumb topping browns and the juices from the pie start to bubble. Remove from the oven and cool on a wire rack.

MANGO, PASSION FRUIT & LIME MERINGUE PIE

SERVINGS: 4

When creating this pie, I wanted the deliciousness of a lemon meringue pie, but with a different fruit base. I love the flavors of tropical fruits. And when my husband and I were in the Dominican Republic on vacation, I ordered a passion fruit cocktail with Brugal rum almost every day. I decided to add the tropical flavors of mango, passion fruit and lime to this meringue pie and the result was better than I could have ever imagined. When you take a bite of this mango passion fruit pie, it will transport you to a tropical sandy beach.

For a full-page photograph of this recipe, see page 52.

PIE CRUST

1 recipe for the single crust Cream Cheese Pie Dough (page 84)

1 large egg + 1 tsp milk or water for egg wash

FILLING

¼ cup (32 g) cornstarch

1⅓ cups (266 g) granulated sugar

5 large egg yolks

½ cup (97 g) mango pulp (frozen and thawed or fresh)

½ cup (97 g) passion fruit pulp (frozen and thawed)

1 tbsp (15 ml) lime juice

1 cup (240 ml) water

1 tbsp (6 g) lime zest

¼ cup (57 g) unsalted butter

FOR THE PIE CRUST: Roll out the pie dough on a lightly floured work surface. The dough should come out about an extra inch from the rim of the pie plate. Place the rolled dough in a 9-inch (23-cm) pie plate. Fold the edges under and crimp them. Use a fork to prick the bottom of the dough. Mix the egg with 1 teaspoon of milk. Brush the egg wash along the perimeter and inside of the pie crust. Place the pie shell in the freezer for about 15 minutes.

Preheat the oven to 375°F (191°C). Once chilled, line the pie dough with a piece of parchment paper and then add pie weights or dry beans into the pie pan. Blind bake the crust for 20 minutes, and then remove the parchment paper and the pie weights. Place the pie pan back into the oven and bake for an additional 15 to 20 minutes, or until the pastry is fully baked and starts to brown slightly. Set the crust aside until ready to use.

FOR THE FILLING: Add the cornstarch and sugar to a medium saucepan. Add the egg yolks, mango and passion fruit pulps, lime juice and water, and then whisk everything together. Place the saucepan over medium-low heat and cook, stirring often, until the filling becomes thick and starts to bubble. This should take 8 minutes.

MERINGUE

5 large egg whites

1¼ cups (250 g) granulated sugar

½ tsp cream of tartar

1 tsp vanilla extract

Remove the filling from the heat and pour it through a fine-mesh strainer into a bowl using a rubber spatula to push it through to remove any bits of egg. Whisk in the lime zest and butter until everything is fully combined.

Pour the mango–passion fruit filling into the prepared pie crust and smooth over the top. Cover the pie with plastic wrap and chill it in the refrigerator for at least 3 hours or overnight.

FOR THE MERINGUE: Add the egg whites, sugar and cream of tartar to the bowl of a stand mixer. Whisk everything together until the mixture is fully combined.

Fill a small pot with about 2 inches (5 cm) of water over medium-high heat. Set the bowl of the stand mixer over the pot of simmering water. Constantly whisk the mixture for 3 to 5 minutes, until the egg whites reach a temperature of 160°F (71°C) and all the sugar has dissolved.

Remove the bowl from the heat and attach the bowl to a stand mixer fitted with a whisk attachment. Turn the mixer on, and gradually increase the speed until it reaches medium-high. Add in the vanilla and whip the meringue for 8 minutes until it is glossy and begins to thicken and forms stiff peaks.

ASSEMBLY: Spoon the meringue on top of the pie filling. Use an offset spatula to spread the meringue around and give it a dome shape while also giving it a wave-like decorative pattern. Use a hand torch to lightly brown the meringue. Chill the pie in the refrigerator until ready to serve.

MIXED BERRY STAR CRUST SLAB PIE

SERVINGS: 4

Every Fourth of July, my great aunt, Marie, made a patriotic dessert like an American flag cake, and I kept up the tradition by making pies with the same theme for the holiday. This mixed berry slab pie has a star-spangled crust design and will be a hit at your Fourth of July get-together or summer barbecue.

SOUR CREAM PIE DOUGH

5 cups (625 g) all-purpose flour

¼ cup (50 g) granulated sugar

2 tsp (12 g) salt

2 cups (456 g) unsalted butter, cubed and frozen (European-style butter, see Note on page 82)

1½ cups (360 ml) sour cream

FILLING

4 cups (592 g) blueberries, fresh or frozen

3 cups (498 g) strawberries, cut up, fresh or frozen

1 cup (140 g) blackberries, fresh or frozen

1 cup (200 g) granulated sugar

3 tbsp (24 g) cornstarch

1 tbsp (15 ml) lemon juice

2 tbsp (12 g) lemon zest

EGG WASH

1 large egg

1 tsp milk or water

TO SERVE

Vanilla ice cream

FOR THE SOUR CREAM PIE DOUGH: Place the flour, sugar and salt in a food processor. Pulse everything to combine. Add the butter and pulse for a few seconds to just combine the flour and fat. Add the sour cream and pulse again until the dough comes together. Divide the dough in half and shape each half into a disk. Wrap each one in plastic wrap and place in the refrigerator for at least an hour or overnight.

Preheat the oven to 375°F (191°C).

FOR THE FILLING: In a large mixing bowl, add the berries, sugar, cornstarch, lemon juice and lemon zest. Mix until all the ingredients are incorporated. Set this aside.

ASSEMBLY: Roll out one pie dough half on a lightly floured work surface, slightly larger than the pie pan. Place the rolled dough in a 9 × 13–inch (23 × 33–cm) quarter-sheet baking pan. Trim and tuck under the excess pie dough. Refrigerate the dough until ready to use.

Roll out the second pie dough. Use differently sized star cookie cutters to cut out the pie dough. Place the cutouts on a baking sheet.

Spread the filling into the dough-lined quarter-sheet pan. Arrange the stars over the filling. Mix the egg with 1 teaspoon of milk. Brush the egg wash along the perimeter of the pie crust. Place the pan in the freezer for 30 minutes.

Bake the slab pie for 45 to 50 minutes or until the crust starts to brown and the filling starts to bubble. Cool on a wire rack and serve with ice cream.

NECTARINE, BLACKBERRY & WALNUT CRISP

SERVINGS: 8

This is such a simple but oh-so-delicious summer dessert! Not sure what to do with those nectarines piled high at the supermarket besides eating them fresh? Turn them into a simple crisp. Crisps are easier to make than pies because they have no bottom crust. There's no pie dough to make, chill or roll out. Just add the sugary fruit to a baking dish and top it with a crumble made of oats, brown sugar, flour and butter. While the crisp bakes in the oven, there is no better aroma!

FILLING

5 nectarines, peeled and cut into chunks

1 cup (140 g) blackberries

⅓ cup (66 g) granulated sugar

1 tbsp (8 g) cornstarch

½ tsp cinnamon

2 tsp (10 ml) lemon juice

1 tsp lemon zest

TOPPING

½ cup (40 g) quick oats

½ cup (63 g) all-purpose flour

½ cup (110 g) packed light brown sugar

¼ cup (29 g) chopped walnuts

½ tsp cinnamon

6 tbsp (84 g) butter

TO SERVE

Vanilla ice cream, optional

Preheat the oven to 350°F (177°C).

FOR THE FILLING: To a medium-sized bowl, add the nectarines, blackberries, granulated sugar, cornstarch, cinnamon, lemon juice and lemon zest. Pour into an 8- or 9-inch (20- or 23-cm), round or square baking dish and set aside.

FOR THE TOPPING: In a small bowl, add the oats, flour, brown sugar, walnuts and cinnamon. Mix together. Add the butter and cut it into the dry ingredients with a fork or with your fingers.

Sprinkle the topping over the fruit. Bake for 50 to 60 minutes until the topping is lightly browned and the filling is bubbly. Serve warm with ice cream, if desired.

SOUR CREAM PIE DOUGH

SERVINGS: 8

I recently discovered the possibility of using sour cream in a pie dough. When I first heard about it, I thought, "How can this be any good?" Replacing cold water or buttermilk with all sour cream? But I gave it a try anyway, and I'm so glad I did! I grew up using only Crisco® shortening in our dough, but this one really steals the show. The result is soft and flaky and perfect for any fruit filling! It's now my main go-to pie dough recipe.

SINGLE CRUST 9-INCH (23-CM) PIE

1¼ cups (156 g) all-purpose flour

1 tbsp (15 g) granulated sugar

½ tsp salt

½ cup (114 g) unsalted butter, cubed and frozen (European-style butter, see Note)

¼ cup + 2 tbsp (90 ml) sour cream

DOUBLE CRUST 9-INCH (23-CM) PIE

2½ cups (312 g) all-purpose flour

2 tbsp (30 g) granulated sugar

1 tsp salt

1 cup (228 g) unsalted butter, cubed and frozen (European-style butter)

¾ cup (180 ml) sour cream

Combine the flour, sugar and salt in a food processor. Pulse to combine all the ingredients. Add the butter and pulse for a few seconds to just combine the flour and fat.

Add the sour cream and pulse again until the dough comes together. Divide the dough in half and shape each half into a disk. Wrap each half in plastic wrap and place them in the refrigerator for an hour or overnight.

NOTE: European butter has a high fat content which is great for pie dough. It contains more fat and less water than regular butter, so it melts faster and makes the crust flakier. I use Kerrygold Pure Irish Unsalted Butter.

CREAM CHEESE PIE DOUGH

SERVINGS: 8

Cream cheese makes for such a great pie dough. It reminds me a lot of a buttery Danish dough. It's flaky with beautiful layers. This recipe uses a combination of cream cheese and a high fat European-style butter, which makes the dough even richer. This dough is perfect for galettes and pies.

SINGLE CRUST 9-INCH (23-CM) PIE

1½ cups (188 g) all-purpose flour

1 tbsp (8 g) cornstarch

1 tsp granulated sugar

½ tsp salt

½ cup (114 g) butter, cubed and frozen (European-style butter, see Note)

4 oz (113 g) cream cheese, cold and cubed

2½ tbsp (37 ml) ice water

1½ tsp (8 ml) apple cider vinegar

DOUBLE CRUST 9-INCH (23-CM) PIE

3 cups (375 g) all-purpose flour

2 tbsp (16 g) cornstarch

2 tsp (10 g) granulated sugar

1 tsp (12 g) salt

1 cup (228 g) butter, cubed and frozen (European-style butter)

8 oz (226 g) cream cheese (1 bar), cold and cubed

¼ cup + 1 tbsp (75 ml) ice water

1 tbsp (15 ml) apple cider vinegar

Combine the flour, cornstarch, sugar and salt in a food processor. Pulse to combine. Add the butter and cream cheese and pulse for a few seconds to just combine the flour and fat.

Combine the ice water and vinegar in a dish. Pour the water mixture into the flour mixture, a little at a time, and pulse again until the dough comes together. Divide the dough in half and shape each half into a disk. Wrap each disk in plastic wrap and place them in the refrigerator for an hour or overnight.

NOTE: European butter has a high fat content which is great for pie dough. It contains more fat and less water than regular butter, so it melts faster and makes the crust flakier. I use Kerrygold Pure Irish Unsalted Butter.

ALL BUTTER PIE DOUGH

SERVINGS: 8

An all butter pie dough is the classic pie dough used by so many. It only uses butter, so it has a great flavor. I also find it to be the easiest dough to make for pie crust decor and lattice crusts.

SINGLE CRUST 9-INCH (23-CM) PIE

1½ cups (188 g) all-purpose flour

1 tbsp (15 g) granulated sugar

¼ tsp salt

½ cup + 3 tbsp (154 g) unsalted butter, cubed and frozen (European-style butter, see Note)

2 tbsp (30 ml) ice cold water (more if necessary)

DOUBLE CRUST 9-INCH (23-CM) PIE

3 cups (375 g) all-purpose flour

2 tbsp (30 g) granulated sugar

½ tsp salt

1¼ cups + 2 tbsp (312 g) unsalted butter, cubed and frozen (European-style butter)

¼ cup (60 ml) ice cold water (more if necessary)

Combine the flour, sugar and salt in a food processor. Pulse to combine. Add the butter and pulse for a few seconds to just combine the flour and fat.

Pour in the ice water, a little at a time, and pulse again until the dough comes together. Divide the dough in half and shape each half into a disk. Wrap each disk in plastic wrap and place them in the refrigerator for an hour or overnight.

NOTE: European butter has a high fat content which is great for pie dough. It contains more fat and less water than regular butter, so it melts faster and makes the crust flakier. I use Kerrygold Pure Irish Unsalted Butter.

LAST-MINUTE TREATS

SOMETIMES, FOR ANY NUMBER OF REASONS, you need to pull together a dessert in a hurry or at the last minute, like that Christmas party potluck that you were supposed to bring something to but totally forgot. Or, perhaps you have company arriving unexpectedly or you want to add another quick dessert to round out your event's celebration menu. Whatever the reason, all hope is not lost! It's definitely possible to make something impressive in an hour or less.

You may have to take a few shortcuts like using store-bought puff pastry, jam or curd; sautéing frozen fruit; or incorporating jarred caramel. Even if an ingredient isn't completely homemade, it can still make your recipe just as delicious.

There have been many times where I had to make a dessert last-minute. Most times, my quick dessert includes brownies. The batter is quick and easy to throw together and everyone loves brownies! There are different ways to make them a little more elegant. One way is adding the brownie batter to a ramekin and making it a molten brownie, like my Deep-Dish Molten Brownie recipe on page 98. The recipe is quick and easy with a beautiful presentation.

There are so many more great last-minute treats in this chapter everyone will love. The Blood Orange Caramel Poached Pears (page 93) is definitely one of my favorites! Who can resist sweet, juicy pears cooked in a rich orange caramel reduction? Of course, I can't forget to mention the Caramelized Piña Colada Pineapples with Coconut Crumble (page 94) and the Peaches en Croûte (page 97). These are all amazing desserts that are made in under an hour and will also definitely be eaten just as quickly!

PEAR TARTE TATIN

SERVINGS: 6

Tarte tatin is a French dessert where fruit is cooked in a pan, a layer of puff pastry is added on top and then the whole dish is baked. It's an easy, delicious, classic dessert that can be put together in under an hour!

PEARS

½ cup (100 g) granulated sugar

2 tbsp (30 ml) water

3 tbsp (42 g) unsalted butter

2 tsp (10 ml) vanilla extract

1 tsp cinnamon

4 small ripe pears

1 (8.6-oz [245-g]) sheet frozen puff pastry, thawed

1 large egg + 1 tsp water for egg wash

TO SERVE

Vanilla ice cream or sweetened whipped cream, optional

Preheat the oven to 375°F (191°C).

FOR THE PEARS: In a 10-inch (25-cm) ovenproof skillet, add the sugar with the water. Cook over medium heat, without stirring, until it begins to turn amber, for 6 to 8 minutes. Add the butter, vanilla and cinnamon, and continue cooking, stirring occasionally, until the mixture is a rich golden color. While the sugar mixture is cooking, peel the pears, slice them in half and remove the cores with a paring knife.

When the sugar mixture is amber, arrange the pear halves in the pan, cut side up. Reduce the heat to medium-low and cook until the pears are slightly tender, about 3 minutes. Turn the pears over cut side down and cook for an additional 2 minutes.

ASSEMBLY: Roll out the puff pastry so that it is a little larger than the original size. Cut the pastry into a circle slightly larger than the size of the pan. Prick the puff pastry with a fork. Place the pastry over the caramelized pears and tuck the edges in.

Combine the egg and water in a small bowl and beat well. With a pastry brush, brush the egg wash all over the top of the puff pastry dough. Bake for 25 to 30 minutes until the pastry is golden brown.

Run a knife around the edge of the skillet, and carefully invert it onto a serving plate. Serve warm, with ice cream, if desired.

MINI PUMPKIN CARAMEL TRIFLES

Pumpkin season basically starts right after Labor Day (although some people like to get started with their pumpkin drinks and recipes in midsummer). This easy pumpkin-layered dessert is quick and simple to make, but will have your guests wanting more!

SERVINGS: 4

12–14 Biscoff® cookies, crushed

1–2 tbsp (14–28 g) unsalted butter, melted

8 oz (226 g) cream cheese, room temperature

1 cup (245 g) canned pumpkin purée

1 tsp vanilla extract

½ cup (100 g) granulated sugar

1 tsp cinnamon

½ tsp nutmeg

1½ cups (240 g) whipped cream topping, divided

4–6 tbsp (85–128 g) caramel topping

In a small dish, combine the Biscoff cookie crumbs and melted butter. Stir to combine. Divide the crumb mixture among four short, 8-ounce (226-ml) Negroni-style glasses, saving some for garnish. Set these aside.

In a medium-sized bowl, add the softened cream cheese, pumpkin purée, vanilla, sugar, cinnamon and nutmeg. Blend with a hand mixer until everything is fully incorporated. Fold in 1 cup (160 g) of the whipped cream topping with a rubber spatula or spoon, just until the pumpkin mixture and whipped topping mix together. Do not over mix.

Divide the mixture evenly among the glasses. Add a tablespoon (21 g) or more of caramel. Garnish with a dollop of whipped cream and a few Biscoff cookie crumbs. Refrigerate until ready to serve.

BLOOD ORANGE CARAMEL POACHED PEARS WITH NUT CRUMBLE

Here's an easy and elegant dessert that takes almost no time at all to make. Lovely ripe pears are simmered in a blood orange caramel poaching liquid and are sprinkled with a pecan crumble to give it just the right amount of crunch to complement the flavorful pears. Add a bit of whipped cream on top to give this dessert the perfect finish.

SERVINGS: 4

POACHED PEARS

¾ cup (150 g) granulated sugar

1½ cups (360 ml) water

½ cup (120 ml) blood orange juice

1 tsp vanilla extract

½ tsp cinnamon

4 ripe pears, peeled, cut in half and cored

NUT CRUMBLE

2 tbsp (16 g) all-purpose flour

2 tbsp (28 g) light brown sugar

¼ cup (27 g) chopped pecans

¼ tsp cinnamon

1 tbsp (14 g) butter

FOR THE POACHED PEARS: Place the granulated sugar in the center of a saucepan large enough to fit all of the pear halves. Heat until the sugar has dissolved, gently stirring with a wooden spoon until the mixture starts to crystallize. It should look clear. Once it reaches this point, do not stir any further. Continue to cook the caramel without stirring until it's amber in color, for 6 to 9 minutes or until the temperature reaches 250°F (121°C) on a candy thermometer.

Once the caramel is an amber color, add the water, blood orange juice, vanilla and cinnamon. Be careful because the caramel will splatter at this point. Simmer for 10 minutes. Add in the pears. Cover and simmer for 10 to 15 minutes or until the pears are tender. Remove the pears and continue to simmer until the caramel has reduced down by about a third.

FOR THE NUT CRUMBLE: Prepare the nut crumble while the pears are simmering. Preheat the oven to 375°F (191°C). Line a baking sheet with parchment paper.

Add the flour, brown sugar, pecans, cinnamon and butter to a small bowl. Press the ingredients together until they are crumbly. Spread out the mixture on the lined baking sheet. Place the crumble into the oven and bake for 5 to 7 minutes. Remove the crumble and allow it to cool.

Place two pear halves in four dishes. Drizzle each pair with the reduced caramel. Divide the nut crumble between the four dishes and serve.

CARAMELIZED PIÑA COLADA PINEAPPLES WITH COCONUT CRUMBLE

Piña coladas are one of my favorite drinks. My mom always ordered one when we would go out for dinner. I thought it was one of the prettiest drinks ever—that creamy drink topped with maraschino cherries, a wedge of pineapple and that cute little colorful paper umbrella! And, once I was of age, I would order piña coladas too. So, I wanted to recreate those piña colada flavors in an easy caramelized pineapple dessert. Adding a little coconut milk to them and some shredded coconut to the crumble did the trick!

SERVINGS: 4

PINEAPPLES
3 tbsp (42 g) butter
½ cup (110 g) brown sugar
½ tsp cinnamon
¼ tsp nutmeg
1 tsp vanilla extract
¼ cup (60 ml) coconut milk
1 tbsp (15 ml) rum
4 fresh pineapple rings

CRUMBLE
3 tbsp (17 g) shredded coconut
2 tsp (10 g) granulated sugar
1 tbsp (14 g) packed light brown sugar
2 tbsp (16 g) all-purpose flour
1 tbsp (14 g) unsalted butter
2 tbsp (15 g) chopped cashews or macadamia nuts

TO SERVE
Coconut or vanilla ice cream, optional

FOR THE PINEAPPLES: Add the butter and brown sugar to a medium-sized skillet over medium heat. Cook until the butter is melted. Add the cinnamon, nutmeg, vanilla, coconut milk and rum. Stir everything together and cook for 2 to 3 minutes. Add the pineapple rings and cook for 3 to 5 minutes on each side. Remove the pineapples and continue to cook the sauce for an additional 2 minutes or until it slightly thickens. Remove from the heat and set aside.

FOR THE CRUMBLE: Preheat the oven to 375°F (191°C). Line a baking sheet with parchment paper.

To a small bowl, add the coconut, granulated sugar, brown sugar and flour. Mix well. Add the butter and cut it in with a fork until the mixture is crumbly. Add the chopped nuts and mix.

Spread the crumble on the lined baking sheet. Bake for 5 to 7 minutes, just until it starts to brown. Remove it from the oven and set aside.

ASSEMBLY: Plate the pineapples and top each with the pan sauce, coconut crumble and a scoop of coconut ice cream, if desired.

PEACHES EN CROÛTE

SERVINGS: 4

En croûte simply translates to "in pastry," and that's just what these are—juicy ripened peaches baked in buttery puff pastry dough with a sugary buttery center. Freestone peaches are the best type of peaches for this recipe because the pit comes out so easily. And the pit needs to be removed so that the center of the peaches can be filled. This dessert is like having a cute mini peach pie!

1 (17.3-oz [490-g]) box frozen puffed pastry sheets, thawed

½ cup (110 g) brown sugar

2 tbsp (28 g) butter

1½ tsp (4 g) cinnamon, divided

¼ tsp nutmeg

4 large very ripe Freestone peaches

¼ cup (50 g) granulated sugar

1 large egg + 1 tsp water for egg wash

Jarred caramel sauce, for serving

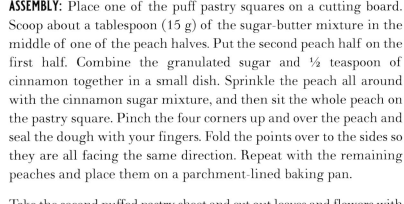

Preheat the oven to 400°F (204°C). Take the thawed puffed pastry out of the box and roll one sheet out slightly larger than the original size. Cut the pastry sheet into four squares. Set them aside.

FOR THE PEACHES: In a bowl, combine the brown sugar, butter, 1 teaspoon of cinnamon and the nutmeg. Refrigerate until ready to use.

Blanch a peach by placing it in boiling water for 45 seconds. Remove the peach and plunge it into ice water to stop the cooking process. Use a paring knife to easily peel the skin off the peach. Find the natural indent of the peach and, starting at the stem, cut the peach in half. Gently twist each side of the peach in opposite directions until the peach pulls apart into two halves. Remove the pit, using a spoon if necessary. Repeat with the other three peaches.

ASSEMBLY: Place one of the puff pastry squares on a cutting board. Scoop about a tablespoon (15 g) of the sugar-butter mixture in the middle of one of the peach halves. Put the second peach half on the first half. Combine the granulated sugar and ½ teaspoon of cinnamon together in a small dish. Sprinkle the peach all around with the cinnamon sugar mixture, and then sit the whole peach on the pastry square. Pinch the four corners up and over the peach and seal the dough with your fingers. Fold the points over to the sides so they are all facing the same direction. Repeat with the remaining peaches and place them on a parchment-lined baking pan.

Take the second puffed pastry sheet and cut out leaves and flowers with cookie plungers/cutters. In a small bowl, beat the egg and water. Brush the egg wash on the pastry-covered peaches. Arrange the cutout leaves and flowers on top. Then, brush the cutouts with the egg wash.

Bake the peaches at 400°F (204°C) for 30 to 40 minutes, until golden brown. Serve with a drizzle of caramel sauce.

DEEP-DISH MOLTEN BROWNIES

SERVINGS: 4

Brownies are one of my favorite desserts ever. For most of my life, I used boxed brownie mix. I mean, it's what my mom always used, so I really didn't think there was any other way to make them. But then, I decided to start making them from scratch. I tested so many recipes over the past few years, and I came up with one that I absolutely love! And in case you're wondering why I included brownies in a book of celebration desserts, it's because whenever it's someone's birthday in my family, we always include brownies. It's simply a tradition for us. These deep-dish molten brownies can be whipped up right away. Unlike traditional brownies, these are baked individually in ramekins, so they bake in only 15 minutes! They are decadent, moist and dense with a soft and smooth liquid chocolate center that flows out when you cut into them.

CHOCOLATE LAVA

1 cup (168 g) semisweet chocolate chips

⅓ cup (80 ml) heavy cream

1 tbsp (14 g) unsalted butter

BROWNIES

½ cup (114 g) butter

¼ cup (125 ml) vegetable oil

3.5 oz (99 g) chocolate bar, chopped

2 large eggs, room temperature

1¼ cups (250 g) granulated sugar

1 tsp vanilla extract

¼ cup + 2 tbsp (30 g) dark cocoa powder

½ tsp salt

½ cup (63 g) all-purpose flour

¼ cup (60 ml) boiling water or coffee

TO SERVE

Vanilla ice cream, optional

FOR THE CHOCOLATE LAVA: Add the chocolate chips, heavy cream and butter to a small saucepan over medium heat. Stir until everything is melted, and then remove the chocolate lava from the heat and pour it into a small bowl. Place in the freezer until ready to use.

FOR THE BROWNIES: Preheat the oven to 425°F (218°C). Spray four 6-ounce (170-g) ramekins with cooking spray.

Add the butter, oil and chopped chocolate to a heatproof bowl over a pot of simmering water. Stir until melted, then remove from the heat. Allow the mixture to cool for 10 to 15 minutes.

While the chocolate mixture is cooling, in a stand mixer or medium-sized mixing bowl with a hand mixer, add the eggs and sugar. Beat for 3 to 5 minutes until the eggs are fluffy and lighter in color.

Fold the melted chocolate mixture into the eggs with a spatula. Add the vanilla and mix again. Add the cocoa powder, salt and flour and stir. Pour in the boiling water and whisk until smooth.

Fill each ramekin halfway with the brownie batter. Remove the chocolate lava from the freezer. Use a cookie scoop or spoon to scoop 1 to 2 tablespoons (15 to 30 ml) of the chocolate lava and place it in the ramekin. Top each ramekin with additional brownie batter, so that the ramekin is filled three-quarters of the way to the top.

Bake for 15 minutes. Remove the brownies from the oven and serve warm with ice cream, if desired.

CHERRY CHEESE TURNOVERS

SERVINGS: 8

These are the perfect little mini treats, especially for the summer holidays. If you want the taste of pie but without the wait of making pie dough and baking for a long time, then this is the dessert for you. This quick and easy treat will make everyone happy.

CHERRY FILLING

3 cups (414 g) fresh cherries, pitted

¼ cup (50 g) granulated sugar

1 tsp lemon juice

¼ cup (60 ml) water

1 tbsp (8 g) cornstarch

CHEESE FILLING

8 oz (226 g) cream cheese, room temperature

¼ cup (50 g) granulated sugar

1 tsp lemon zest

PASTRY

1 (17.3-oz [490-g]) box frozen puff pastry sheets, thawed

1 egg + 1 tsp water

¼ cup (51 g) turbinado sugar

FOR THE CHERRY FILLING: In a saucepan over medium heat, place the cherries, granulated sugar, lemon juice, water and cornstarch. Cook until the cherries start to soften and the mixture thickens, for 10 minutes. Remove the cherry filling from the heat and transfer it to a bowl to cool completely. Then, place it in a second bowl of ice water to cool faster.

FOR THE CHEESE FILLING: In a medium bowl, place the cream cheese, granulated sugar and lemon zest. Beat with a hand mixer until it is smooth.

ASSEMBLY: On a lightly floured work surface, roll out one of the puff pastry sheets. Cut it into four squares. Use a small cookie cutter to cut out a shape on one side of the dough. On the other side, add 1 to 1½ tablespoons (15 to 23 g) of the cheese filling. Add about 1 tablespoon (15 g) of the cherry filling on top.

Whisk the egg and water in a small dish to make the egg wash. Brush the egg wash on the border of the pastry square. Fold the half with the cutout over the half with the filling. Seal the edges with a fork.

Repeat the process with the second puff pastry sheet. Brush the tops of the turnovers with the egg wash and sprinkle turbinado sugar generously on top.

Preheat the oven to 425°F (218°C) and place the turnovers in the refrigerator while the oven heats. Bake for 15 to 20 minutes or until the pastries have browned.

PUFF PASTRY APPLE TARTS

SERVINGS: 9

I love all apple desserts. Apple pie is such a classic and these apple tarts encompass everything you love about apple pie, but in a much easier and quicker dessert. Using buttery puff pastry speeds up the process but still keeps the deliciousness. Cut the pastry into squares, add sliced apples, sugar and spices and you have a delicious mini version of the classic apple pie.

CRUMB TOPPING

¼ cup (31 g) all-purpose flour

3 tbsp (42 g) dark brown sugar

½ tsp cinnamon

2 tbsp (28 g) unsalted butter, cold

APPLE FILLING

3 large apples, any variety

3 tbsp (45 g) granulated sugar

¼ tsp cinnamon

½ tsp vanilla extract

TARTS

1 (8.6-oz [245-g]) sheet frozen puff pastry, thawed

1 egg + 1 tbsp (15 ml) water

3 tbsp (168 g) apple jelly, to glaze

Preheat the oven to 375°F (191°C).

FOR THE CRUMB TOPPING: Add the flour, brown sugar and cinnamon to a small mixing bowl and stir. Add the butter and press it into the mixture with your fingers until the mixture is crumbly. Place the bowl into the refrigerator until ready to use.

FOR THE APPLE FILLING: Cut each apple in half, leaving on the skin, if desired. Core the center, and then cut each half into thin slices. Place the slices in a bowl and add the granulated sugar, cinnamon and vanilla. Toss the apples gently until they are coated. Set the filling aside.

ASSEMBLY: On a lightly floured work surface, roll out the sheet of puff pastry with a rolling pin until the sheet gets about a ½ inch (1.3 cm) larger on all sides. Cut the puff pastry sheet into nine equally-sized squares with a pizza cutter or sharp knife and place them on a large baking sheet lined with parchment paper. Whisk together the egg and water until blended, and then lightly brush each square with the egg wash.

Top each square with about four to five slices of the apples in a row, with the apples overlapping slightly. Add about a ½ teaspoon of crumble to each tartlet. Repeat with the remaining pastry squares.

Place the pan in the oven and bake for 15 to 25 minutes, or until the puff pastry puffs up around the edges and turns golden brown.

Add the apple jelly to a small saucepan and heat until it is melted. Brush each pastry with the jelly. Serve immediately.

ORANGE RUM CHEESECAKE TRIFLES

SERVINGS: 4

Since citrus season starts during the winter, making an orange-flavored dessert during the holidays is perfect! These Orange Rum Cheesecake Trifles will be a showstopper on your dessert table and the addition of rum gives it just the kick it needs!

CLEMENTINES

¼ cup (50 g) granulated sugar

2 tbsp (30 ml) water

2 tbsp (30 ml) white rum

4 clementine oranges, peeled and cut into wedges

CRUMBLE

1 cup (84 g) crushed shortbread or butter cookies, like Lorna Doone®

3 tbsp (42 g) unsalted butter, melted

FILLING

¾ cup (180 g) heavy cream

¼ cup (30 g) confectioners' sugar

8 oz (226 g) cream cheese, room temperature

2 tbsp (30 ml) frozen orange juice concentrate, thawed

1 tsp orange zest

GARNISH

Whipped cream

Orange zest

FOR THE CLEMENTINES: Place the sugar, water and rum in a sauté pan. Bring to a simmer over medium heat and cook for 3 to 4 minutes, just until the sugar has fully dissolved and the liquid looks clear. Add the clementine wedges and cook for an additional 4 to 5 minutes to incorporate the fruit into the liquid. Remove the clementines from the heat and cool them completely. The liquid will thicken slightly, similar to a simple syrup. Set them aside until ready to use.

FOR THE CRUMBLE: Mix together the crushed cookies and melted butter. Refrigerate the crumble mixture while preparing the filling.

FOR THE FILLING: Combine the heavy cream and confectioners' sugar in a medium-sized mixing bowl. Using a hand mixer, beat on medium-high for 2 minutes, or until soft peaks form. Add the softened cream cheese. Blend on medium-low until smooth. Add the thawed concentrated orange juice and beat on low until everything is combined. Add the orange zest and beat on medium-high for 2 minutes until the filling is smooth, light and airy.

ASSEMBLY: Divide the shortbread mixture among four glasses. Add the filling to a pastry bag. Cut off the tip so that there is a 1-inch (2.5-cm) opening. Pipe the filling nearly halfway to the top. Add two to three of the clementine wedges on top of the filling.

Garnish with the whipped cream and orange zest. Refrigerate until ready to serve.

STRAWBERRY LEMON NAPOLEONS

SERVINGS: 6

The Napoleon is a classic French dessert that consists of flaky puff pastry layers, usually with thick layers of pastry cream. In my version, I wanted to make a quick dessert by layering cream cheese whipped cream, lemon curd and plenty of plump sweet strawberries in baked puff pastry sheets. This Napoleon is the best indulgence!

PASTRY
2 (17.3-oz [490-g]) sheets store-bought puff pastry, thawed

CREAM CHEESE WHIPPED CREAM
8 oz (226 g) cream cheese, room temperature

1 cup (120 g) confectioners' sugar

1 tsp vanilla extract

2 cups (480 ml) heavy cream, cold

FILLING
2 tbsp (108 g) jarred lemon curd

1½ cups (249 g) sliced strawberries

GARNISH
2 tbsp (3 g) crushed freeze-dried strawberries

FOR THE PASTRY: Preheat the oven to 400°F (204°C). Cut each puff pastry sheet into six equal-sized rectangles, so that you have twelve rectangles in total.

Prick the pastry all over with a fork and transfer to two parchment-lined baking sheets. Top the pastry rectangles with another sheet of parchment paper, and then place another baking sheet on top of each set of pastries. Bake on two oven racks for 15 to 20 minutes. If you only have two baking sheets instead of four, bake the pastries in two batches. Remove the pans from the oven and cool the pastry on wire racks.

FOR THE CREAM CHEESE WHIPPED CREAM: In a stand mixer with the whisk attachment or a bowl with a hand mixer, beat the cream cheese, confectioners' sugar and vanilla until the mixture is smooth and thick.

While mixing on medium-high speed, slowly add the heavy cream. Continue whipping until it forms stiff peaks. It will resemble whipped cream but will be thicker. Add the frosting to a pastry bag with a round tip or cut about an inch off the tip of the bag and set it aside.

ASSEMBLY: Place 1 pastry rectangle on a dessert plate and spread 1 teaspoon of lemon curd evenly on top. Add a layer of strawberry slices. Pipe dollops of the whipped cream frosting on top of the strawberries. Add a second pastry on top. Add additional sliced strawberries and dollop another layer of the whipped cream. Repeat with the rest of the pastry rectangles and filling so you have six total Napoleons. Using a mesh strainer, sprinkle some crushed freeze-dried strawberries on top. Serve immediately.

AHEAD

WHEN YOU HAVE A BIG EVENT COMING UP OR THE HOLIDAYS with a lot of family and friends, you want to save as much time in the kitchen as you can. One helpful way to do that is to make some of your desserts ahead of time. That way, you can spend a little extra time getting the house together, setting the table or even relaxing!

Some desserts are more suited to making ahead than others, mostly because you want them to "set." In other words, after the dessert is made, it may be too soft to serve right away. Placing it in the refrigerator or freezer for some time will help it to firm up or become more solid, in turn giving the dessert a wonderfully smooth texture!

Another make-ahead method is to freeze a baked and cooled dessert, ensuring you have a delightful dessert on hand at any moment! My grandmother was famous for baking her delicious butter pound cake, slicing it after it cooled, individually wrapping the slices and placing them in the freezer so we could enjoy a slice any time we wanted to. Because it was wrapped so well, the cake stayed fresh and delicious. This can easily be done with my Southern Meyer Lemon Pound Cake on page 127.

All of the recipes in this chapter are perfect to make ahead of time like the White Chocolate Bread Pudding (page 115) and the Mango Lime Sorbet (page 116). Also, I included one of my favorite desserts, the Salted Caramel Crème Brûlée on page 123. The Crème Brûlée is rich and creamy with a delicious caramel base. I can never say no to salted caramel. But really, who can?

SWEET POTATO CHEESECAKE WITH GINGER SNAP CRUST

SERVINGS: 10

If you love sweet potato pie, then you will love this sweet potato pie cheesecake! I first made this recipe years ago one Thanksgiving when I was planning the dessert menu. I knew I wanted to make a cheesecake, because we all love cheesecake in my family. But, I didn't want to make a plain one. I wanted a cheesecake with a special flavor. Someone suggested that since it was for Thanksgiving, I should try adding sweet potatoes. It was such a great idea because sweet potato pie was one of my favorites, so why not combine the two? The result was fantastic! And I started making this sweet potato cheesecake regularly.

CRUST

2 cups (168 g) ginger snap crumbs, crushed in a food processor

½ cup (55 g) finely chopped pecans

⅓ cup (66 g) granulated sugar

½ cup (114 g) butter, melted

FILLING

4 (8-oz [226-g]) cream cheese blocks, room temperature

1⅓ cups (293 g) light brown sugar

2½ cups (620 g) plain mashed sweet potatoes (2–3 baked sweet potatoes)

2 tsp (10 ml) vanilla extract

2 large eggs, room temperature

1 cup (240 ml) heavy cream, room temperature

½ cup (120 ml) sour cream, room temperature

1 tsp cinnamon

½ tsp nutmeg

FOR THE CRUST: Preheat the oven to 350°F (177°C). Wrap a 9-inch (23-cm) springform pan with aluminum foil.

In a medium-sized bowl, combine the ginger snap crumbs, pecans, granulated sugar and melted butter. Mix well. Pour the crumbs into the spring-form pan and press them firmly into the bottom and up the sides of the pan. Set aside.

FOR THE FILLING: In a stand mixer with a paddle attachment or a large bowl with a hand mixer, beat the cream cheese and brown sugar until the mixture is creamy. Add the mashed sweet potatoes, vanilla and eggs. Beat until they are smooth. Add the heavy cream, sour cream, cinnamon and nutmeg. Blend until all the ingredients are incorporated.

ASSEMBLY: Pour the filling into the springform pan. Place the pan into a larger pan. Fill the outer pan halfway with water and place the pans in the oven. Bake for 1 hour to 1 hour and 10 minutes. Turn off the heat and let the cheesecake sit in the oven for an additional 30 minutes so the residual heat continues to cook it.

Remove the pan from the water and set the cheesecake on a wire rack. Let it cool to room temperature. Cover and refrigerate it for at least 3 hours or up to 4 days.

When ready to serve, run a sharp knife around the edge of the pan, remove the outer ring and serve.

CHERRY PISTACHIO CHEESECAKE TERRINE

SERVINGS: 8

Cherries and pistachios are a classic pairing and they work together beautifully in this delicious terrine. The base is a no-churn ice cream with cherry and pistachio notes running through it. It's rich and creamy and a great dessert to make a day a two before you plan to serve it.

CHERRY PURÉE

3 cups (414 g) fresh or frozen pitted cherries

1 tbsp (15 g) granulated sugar

2 tbsp (30 ml) water

TERRINE

1 (14-oz [392-g]) can sweetened condensed milk

8 oz (226 g) cream cheese

1 tbsp (15 ml) vanilla extract

2 cups (480 ml) cold heavy cream

Prepared cherry purée, divided

2 tbsp (13 g) chopped pistachios

GARNISH

Fresh cherries

Chopped pistachios

FOR THE CHERRY PURÉE: Add the cherries, sugar and water to a saucepan. Cook for 7 to 10 minutes or until the cherries start to soften. Remove the saucepan from the heat and allow to cool. Add the cherries and juice from the saucepan to a high-powered blender and purée. Set aside until ready to use.

FOR THE TERRINE: In a large mixing bowl, combine the condensed milk, cream cheese and vanilla. Beat until smooth.

In a separate mixing bowl, whip the heavy cream until stiff peaks form. Fold the whipped cream into the condensed milk mixture. Then fold in half of the puréed cherries and the chopped pistachios.

ASSEMBLY: Line a large loaf pan with plastic wrap, making sure that all of the sides are covered and some of the plastic hangs out of the pan. Pour the mixture into the loaf pan. Add the remaining cherry purée by the spoonful. Swirl it with a knife to create swirls of cherry purée throughout the mixture. Cover the loaf pan with additional plastic wrap and place it into the freezer for at least 6 hours or overnight, until it is solid.

To serve, invert the terrine onto a serving platter, peel off all of the plastic, and garnish it with cherries and chopped pistachios.

WHITE CHOCOLATE BREAD PUDDING

SERVINGS: 8

Bread pudding is such a great dessert. It's usually made with day-old, stale challah or brioche bread, but for this recipe, I decided to use croissants. The buttery soft layers of the croissant make for such a delicious bread pudding. Adding white chocolate makes this rich, buttery bread pudding even better! Make this dish ahead of time by putting the whole thing together, covering and refrigerating it overnight, and then bake it the next day.

BREAD PUDDING

6 large 1–2 day-old croissants

2 (4-oz [113-g]) white chocolate bars

3 whole large eggs

3 large egg yolks

1½ cups (360 ml) heavy cream

¾ cup (180 ml) whole milk

¾ cup (150 g) granulated sugar

¼ tsp cinnamon

2 tsp (4 g) orange zest

1 tbsp (15 ml) vanilla extract

Butter, for greasing dish

KENTUCKY BOURBON SAUCE

1 cup (240 ml) heavy cream

½ cup (120 ml) milk or half and half

½ cup (100 g) granulated sugar

1 tsp vanilla extract

1–2 tbsp (8–16 g) cornstarch

¼ cup (60 ml) Kentucky bourbon

GARNISH

Orange zest

FOR THE BREAD PUDDING: Preheat the oven to 350°F (177°F). Cut the croissants into small cubes, place them in a large bowl and set them aside.

In a heatproof bowl, add the white chocolate. Place it over a small saucepan filled one-third full with simmering water, making sure the bottom of the bowl does not touch the water. Stir the chocolate with a rubber spatula until it is fully melted. Set this aside.

In a bowl, add the eggs, egg yolks, heavy cream, milk, sugar, cinnamon, orange zest and vanilla, and then add the melted white chocolate. Whisk until all the ingredients are incorporated. Pour the mixture on top of the bread cubes. Stir until all of the pieces are completely coated.

Grease a casserole dish with butter. Add the bread pudding to the casserole dish and cover it with aluminum foil. Place the bread pudding into a larger pan and place it in the oven. Pour enough water into the larger pan so that it comes halfway up the casserole dish. Bake for 30 to 35 minutes. Remove the foil and bake for an additional 15 to 20 minutes, until the pudding is puffed and browning. Carefully remove the pan from the oven and allow it to cool slightly.

FOR THE KENTUCKY BOURBON SAUCE: While the bread pudding is baking, add the heavy cream, milk, sugar and vanilla to a saucepan. Bring the mixture to a simmer. Combine the cornstarch and bourbon in a small dish. Add to the warmed cream and whisk until it is thickened.

Garnish the bread pudding with orange zest and serve with the bourbon sauce.

MANGO LIME SORBET

Sorbet is such a simple dessert that packs such a big punch of flavor! It has very few ingredients, but tastes so amazing. And for this sorbet, the mango is the star of the show. It's tropical, cool, and so refreshing. Because this sorbet has to set overnight in the freezer, it's the perfect treat to make a day or more ahead of time. And when you're ready to serve the sorbet, it's already done! This is the dessert that you'll want to have at a summer party.

5 cups (700 g) frozen mango chunks, or 4 large ripe mangos, peeled, pit removed and cut into chunks

¾ cup (150 g) granulated sugar

1 tbsp (6 g) lime zest

⅓ cup (80 ml) fresh lime juice

¾ cup (180 ml) water (or more if needed)

If you're using fresh mangos, add the mango chunks to a lidded container and freeze overnight.

Add the frozen mango pieces, sugar, lime zest, lime juice and water to a food processor or a high-powered blender. Blend until the mixture is smooth. Add additional water if needed to make the mixture smooth.

Spoon the mixture into a medium-sized dish, cover with plastic wrap and freeze for at least 4 hours or overnight until firm. Scoop the sorbet into cones or dessert dishes to serve.

BROWNIE ICE CREAM CAKE

SERVINGS: 16

Growing up, anytime we had a holiday party at school I always asked my mom to bake brownies to bring in. Boxed brownies were so good! Now, I've come up with my own brownie recipe as close as I could to the deliciousness of boxed brownies. And to elevate them even further, I've made them into an amazing ice cream cake. With layers of brownies, ganache and ice cream, this is the best summer treat!

BROWNIE LAYER

½ cup (114 g) butter

½ cup (120 ml) vegetable oil

3.5 oz (99 g) unsweetened chocolate bar, chopped

2 large eggs, room temperature

1¼ cups (250 g) granulated sugar

1 tsp vanilla extract

¼ cup + 2 tbsp (32 g) dark cocoa powder

½ tsp salt

½ cup (63 g) all-purpose flour

¼ cup (60 ml) boiling water or coffee

MIDDLE LAYER

½ cup (120 ml) heavy cream

1 cup (168 g) dark chocolate chips

6–8 Oreo cookies, finely crumbled

ICE CREAM LAYER

1.5 quarts (1.4 L) ice cream of your choice (I used raspberry), slightly softened

1 cup (160 g) whipped topping

FOR THE BROWNIE LAYER: Preheat the oven to 350°F (177°C). Cut a piece of parchment paper to fit a 9-inch (23-cm), round baking pan and place it in the bottom. Spray the inner sides of the pan with baking spray.

Add the butter, oil and chopped chocolate to a heatproof bowl over a shallow pot of simmering water. Stir until everything is melted, and then remove it from the heat. Allow the mixture to cool for 10 to 15 minutes.

In a stand mixer or a medium-sized mixing bowl with a hand mixer, add the eggs and sugar. Beat for 3 to 5 minutes until the eggs are fluffy and paler in color. Fold the melted chocolate mixture into the eggs with a spatula. Add the vanilla and mix again. Add the cocoa powder, salt and flour and stir. Pour in the boiling water and whisk until smooth.

Pour the batter into the pan and bake for 20 minutes. Remove from the oven and allow the brownie to cool completely.

ASSEMBLY: Remove the brownie from the pan and peel off the parchment paper. Place it in a 9-inch (23-cm) springform pan.

Heat the heavy cream in a saucepan until it is very hot, but do not let it boil. Meanwhile, add the chocolate chips to a heatproof bowl. Pour the hot cream over the chocolate and allow the mixture to sit for 1 to 2 minutes to melt. Stir with a spoon until smooth.

Pour the chocolate ganache mixture over the brownie. Sprinkle the crushed Oreo cookies in an even layer on top. Spread the ice cream over the cookies. Spread the whipped topping on top of the ice cream. Cover with plastic wrap and freeze for 4 hours or overnight.

Remove the sides from the springform pan, transfer the ice cream cake to a serving plate or cake stand and serve.

BAILEY'S CHOCOLATE MOUSSE

SERVINGS: 6

When I think of smooth and creamy desserts, the first two things that come to mind are pudding and mousse. Mousse is the lighter, fluffier cousin of pudding. Its lighter texture comes from whipping air into the mixture. The result is a chocolatey, fluffy, delicious dessert! Adding a touch of Bailey's® Irish Cream gives it that boozy kick that makes it just right.

CHOCOLATE MOUSSE

4 large egg yolks

⅓ cup (66 g) granulated sugar

2½ cups (600 ml) heavy cream, divided

2 (3.5-oz [99-g]) bars dark chocolate, chopped

⅛ tsp salt

2 tsp (10 ml) vanilla extract

½ cup (120 ml) Bailey's Irish Cream

BAILEY'S WHIPPED CREAM

1 cup (240 ml) heavy cream

¼ cup (30 g) confectioners' sugar

¼ cup (60 ml) Bailey's Irish Cream

FOR THE CHOCOLATE MOUSSE: In a medium-sized bowl with a hand mixer, whip the egg yolks and granulated sugar on high speed for 2 to 3 minutes, until the mixture is pale and thick.

Heat 1 cup (240 ml) of the heavy cream in a small saucepan over low heat. While whisking the egg mixture slowly, pour in the warm cream mixture a little at a time, to temper the egg yolks. Keep whisking the mixture between each pour. Then, pour everything back into the saucepan. Cook over low heat, whisking constantly for 3 to 5 minutes, until the mixture thickens just slightly. Remove from the heat.

Add in the chopped chocolate and salt and stir until it is fully incorporated. Place a mesh strainer over a medium-sized bowl and pour the mixture through the strainer. Use a rubber spatula to press the mixture through to remove any small pieces of cooked egg. Add the vanilla and Bailey's Irish Cream. Let the mixture cool to room temperature, but do not let it get cold.

Once it is cooled to room temperature, in a separate medium bowl, add the remaining 1½ cups (360 ml) of heavy cream and beat with a hand mixer until it reaches stiff peaks. Use a rubber spatula to gently fold the whipped cream into the chocolate custard mixture. Divide the mousse evenly among six 8-ounce (226-ml) dessert glasses. Refrigerate the mousse until ready to serve.

FOR THE BAILEY'S WHIPPED CREAM: Add the heavy cream, confectioners' sugar and Bailey's Irish Cream to a medium-sized bowl. With a hand mixer, beat the cream until it forms stiff peaks.

Top the chocolate mousse with whipped cream and serve.

SALTED CARAMEL CRÈME BRÛLÉE

SERVINGS: 6

Crème brûlée is one of my favorite desserts! The creaminess of the dessert with the crackling sugar top sends me over the edge. The day I graduated from graduate school, my family and I went to a great restaurant on the west side of Manhattan to eat first. After we had dinner, I spotted a great crème brûlée on the menu, but before I could order, we realized it was time to get to the graduation because the ceremony was to start soon. I was so disappointed that I didn't get to end that meal with the crème brûlée. That's the day I realized how much I loved this rich and creamy dessert. So, I stopped back by the restaurant after the graduation to get that crème brûlée "to go" after the ceremony was over. I had to have it! And that's why I love making crème brûlée at home. I can have it anytime. This version starts with a salted caramel base before the rich custard is added to make this crème brûlée ultra creamy and delicious!

¾ cup (150 g) granulated sugar
¼ cup + 2 tbsp (90 ml) water
3 cups (720 ml) heavy cream
¾ tsp salt
1 tbsp (15 ml) vanilla extract
6 large egg yolks
6 tbsp (35 g) fine sugar

FOR THE CARAMEL: Place the granulated sugar and water in a stainless steel saucepan over low heat. Cook until the sugar is dissolved and the caramel turns amber in color. Do not stir. Slowly pour in the heavy cream and whisk until the caramel is smooth. Remove the saucepan from the heat and stir in the salt and vanilla.

FOR THE CUSTARD: In a bowl with a hand mixer, beat the egg yolks for 1 to 2 minutes until the mixture is pale and thick. While mixing, slowly pour in the warm caramel mixture a little at a time, to temper the egg yolks. Once fully mixed, strain the mixture through a mesh strainer into a large measuring cup, and then pour it equally into six 6-ounce (170-g) ramekins.

ASSEMBLY: Preheat the oven to 325°F (163°C). Place the ramekins on a baking pan and place the pan into the oven. Pour hot water in the baking pan, halfway up the sides of the ramekins. Bake the ramekins for 45 minutes or until the centers look just set.

Remove the ramekins from the baking pan and set them on a cooling rack to cool to room temperature for about an hour. Cover each ramekin with plastic wrap and place them into the refrigerator to set, for at least 4 hours or up to 3 days.

When ready to serve, sprinkle the fine sugar evenly over the tops of each crème brûlée. Use a hand torch to caramelize the sugar on top.

PINEAPPLE CHEESECAKE

SERVINGS: 10

My mother made pineapple cheese pie numerous times while I was growing up and I loved it. It was essentially a no-bake cheesecake using cream cheese and condensed milk topped with sweetened pineapples. I decided to give the vintage cheese pie dessert a modern makeover by making it a creamy vanilla cheesecake topped with a layer of homemade pineapple jam. If you love creative cheesecakes, you will definitely want to try this out!

PINEAPPLE JAM
2 cups (300 g) diced fresh pineapples

⅓ cup (65 g) packed light brown sugar

1 tbsp (15 ml) lemon juice

2 tbsp (30 ml) pineapple juice or water

2 tsp (5 g) cornstarch

CRUST
2 cups (168 g) graham cracker crumbs

¼ cup (50 g) granulated sugar

½ cup (114 g) butter, melted

FILLING
4 (8-oz [226-g]) blocks cream cheese, room temperature

1⅓ cups (266 g) granulated sugar

1 tsp vanilla extract

1 tsp lemon juice

2 large eggs, room temperature

1 cup (240 ml) heavy cream, room temperature

½ cup (120 ml) sour cream, room temperature

GARNISH
Whipped cream, optional

FOR THE PINEAPPLE JAM: Add the diced pineapples, brown sugar, lemon juice, pineapple juice and cornstarch to a saucepan. Cook over medium heat until the pineapples soften and the jam thickens slightly. Remove from the heat and allow it to cool completely. Place the jam into the refrigerator until ready to use.

FOR THE CRUST: Preheat the oven to 350°F (177°C). Wrap a 9-inch (23-cm) springform pan with aluminum foil.

In a medium-sized bowl, combine the graham cracker crumbs, granulated sugar and melted butter. Mix well. Pour the crumbs into the springform pan and press firmly into the bottom and up the sides of the pan. Set this aside.

FOR THE FILLING: In a stand mixer with a paddle attachment or a large bowl with a hand mixer, beat the cream cheese and granulated sugar until creamy. Add the vanilla, lemon juice and eggs. Beat until smooth. Add the heavy cream and sour cream, and blend until all the ingredients are incorporated.

ASSEMBLY: Pour the filling into the springform pan. Place the pan into a larger pan. Fill the outer pan halfway with water and place the pans in the oven. Bake for an hour to 1 hour and 10 minutes. Turn off the heat and let the cheesecake sit in the oven for an additional 30 minutes so the residual heat continues to cook it.

Remove the pan from the water and set the cheesecake on a wire rack. Let it cool to room temperature. Cover and refrigerate for at least 3 hours or up to 4 days. When ready to serve, run a sharp knife around the edge of the pan, remove the outer ring and place the cheesecake on a serving platter. Spread the pineapple jam on top. Garnish with whipped cream dollops around the top of the cheesecake, if desired.

SOUTHERN MEYER LEMON POUND CAKE

SERVINGS: 12

I grew up eating pound cake all the time. My grandmother would bake it, individually wrap slices and put them in the freezer. So, when we wanted a slice, she would take it out of the freezer and warm it in the oven. Those were the best times! She would often add an extra flavoring to her cake like almond or lemon extract. This inspired me to make a lemon pound cake—and not just any lemon pound cake, but a Meyer lemon pound cake. Meyer lemons are a cross between a lemon and a mandarin. They are more orange in color and have a more mellow, sweet taste than regular lemons, and they give this pound cake the most delicious citrus flavor!

POUND CAKE

1½ cups (341 g) butter, room temperature

2½ cups (300 g) granulated sugar

6 large eggs, room temperature

2 tsp (10 ml) vanilla extract

1 tbsp (15 ml) fresh Meyer lemon juice (juice from regular lemons can be substituted if needed)

1 tbsp (6 g) Meyer lemon zest

3 cups (375 g) all-purpose flour

½ tsp salt

1 tsp baking powder

1 cup (240 ml) sour cream, room temperature

LEMON GLAZE

2 cups (240 g) confectioners' sugar

2 tbsp (30 ml) Meyer lemon juice

1–2 tbsp (15–30 ml) whole milk, divided

GARNISH

A mix of fresh berries

FOR THE CAKE: Preheat the oven to 350°F (177°C). Spray both parts of a 10-inch (25-cm) tube pan with baking spray.

In a stand mixer with a paddle attachment or a large bowl with a hand mixer, cream together the butter and granulated sugar. Add the eggs, vanilla, Meyer lemon juice and zest. Mix until everything is incorporated. Add the flour, salt, baking powder and sour cream. Mix again.

Pour the batter into the prepared tube pan. Bake for 60 to 70 minutes, or until a toothpick inserted into the middle comes out clean. Cool on a wire rack.

FOR THE LEMON GLAZE: In a bowl, add the confectioners' sugar, lemon juice and 1 tablespoon (15 ml) of milk. Mix well until the glaze is smooth. Add the additional tablespoon (15 ml) of milk if the glaze seems too thick.

Drizzle the lemon glaze on top of the pound cake, slice and serve with fresh berries.

NOTE: The cake can be wrapped well in plastic wrap and aluminum foil and frozen up to 3 months until ready to serve.

PINK GRAPEFRUIT POSSETS

SERVINGS: 4

The posset is a dessert that I recently discovered and I absolutely love. It's so simple to make by simply cooking sweetened cream and adding a little citrus. Most versions of this dessert are lemon-flavored, but for this recipe, I used pink grapefruit. I love the sweet and bitter taste of grapefruits compared to the sourness of lemons. It works so well in this posset and by adding a little gelee to the top, it becomes a beautiful eye-catching dessert!

GRAPEFRUIT POSSET

2 cups (480 ml) heavy cream
⅔ cup (132 g) granulated sugar
½ tsp vanilla extract
¼ cup (60 ml) grapefruit juice
1 tbsp (6 g) grapefruit zest

GELEE

2 tsp (10 ml) cold water
1 tsp gelatin
¾ cup (180 ml) freshly squeezed grapefruit juice
1 tbsp (15 g) granulated sugar
1 grapefruit, segmented

FOR THE GRAPEFRUIT POSSET: In a saucepan over medium heat, warm the heavy cream, sugar and vanilla. Let it come to a simmer for 3 minutes. Let the mixture gently bubble as it simmers, but do not allow it to reach a full boil.

Remove the cream from the heat and stir in the grapefruit juice and grapefruit zest. Allow the posset to cool for about 10 minutes.

FOR THE GELEE: Add the cold water into a small bowl. Sprinkle the gelatin over the water and allow it to bloom for 5 minutes.

In a small saucepan, heat the grapefruit juice and sugar. Once it comes to a simmer, add the bloomed gelatin and whisk until it has fully dissolved. Remove it from the heat. Let it cool for about 10 minutes.

ASSEMBLY: Divide the cream between four 6-ounce (170-ml) jars or glasses. Refrigerate the possets for about 3 hours. Place two to three segmented grapefruit slices on top of each one. Pour the grapefruit gelee on top of the grapefruit pieces in the jars.

Allow the posset to chill for at least 1 hour or overnight.

SIMPLE & ELEGANT BITE-SIZED BAKES

IS THERE ANYTHING BETTER THAN A RICH AND DECADENT HOMEMADE DESSERT? When it is made into a smaller version, it somehow becomes even more desirable. From tea cakes to cupcakes to macarons, these mini desserts prove that bite-sized is just as delicious as a larger dessert.

I have to admit, small-sized desserts have always been a favorite of mine. Having a variety of several mini desserts as opposed to one large one is just amazing. You get a little bit of everything!

This chapter includes some really delicious mini treats. One of my favorite treats are cupcakes. Be it birthdays, showers or holidays, I'll take a really great cupcake every time, especially with creative flavors such as the Pineapple Mojito Cupcakes on page 133—vanilla cupcakes with pineapple curd topped with pineapple buttercream and a pineapple "flower." So cute and yummy! There's also Citrus Madeleines (page 159) and the delicate but oh-so-delectable Raspberry White Chocolate Macaron (page 149)! All of the amazing bite-sized treats in this chapter are classic desserts I know you will love!

PINEAPPLE MOJITO CUPCAKES

**SERVINGS:
12 TO 14 CUPCAKES**

This recipe came about because I love using dried fruit as a garnish. And when you slice and dry out pineapple slices, they look like beautiful flowers. So, I had to make a cupcake flavor to go with the pineapple flowers. Pineapple and mojito are a tropical match made in heaven—it's such a fun flavor twist in these delightful cupcakes!

PINEAPPLE CURD

4 large egg yolks

⅓ cup (66 g) granulated sugar

⅓ cup (80 ml) pineapple juice or nectar

1 tbsp (8 g) cornstarch

2 tbsp (30 ml) heavy cream

¼ cup + 2 tbsp (84 g) butter

CUPCAKES

2 large egg whites, room temperature

1 cup (200 g) granulated sugar

2 tbsp (28 g) butter, room temperature

¼ cup (60 ml) vegetable oil

1 tsp vanilla extract

¼ cup (60 ml) buttermilk, room temperature

¼ cup (60 ml) sour cream, room temperature

1½ cups (188 g) all-purpose flour

1½ tsp (7 g) baking powder

½ tsp baking soda

½ tsp salt

FOR THE PINEAPPLE CURD: In a small saucepan, place the egg yolks, sugar, pineapple juice, cornstarch and heavy cream, and whisk by hand to combine. Cook the mixture over low to medium heat, whisking constantly, until the mixture becomes thick, for 5 to 10 minutes.

Remove the curd from the heat and immediately strain it through a fine-mesh sieve over a bowl by pushing the curd with a spoon or rubber spatula. Discard any small pieces of cooked egg left in the sieve. Add the butter and whisk until it's completely melted. Place the curd in an airtight container and refrigerate it for at least 2 hours or overnight.

FOR THE CUPCAKES: Preheat the oven to 350°F (177°C). Line a 12-cup muffin pan with liners. Add two additional liners to another muffin pan if making more than twelve.

In a stand mixer with the paddle attachment or a large mixing bowl with a hand mixer, add the egg whites and granulated sugar. Beat until the mixture is thick and fluffy, for 2 minutes. Add the butter and oil, and then mix again. Add the vanilla, buttermilk and sour cream and blend together. Add the flour, baking powder, baking soda and salt and blend until smooth.

Scoop the batter into the pan, filling the wells halfway to three-quarters full. Bake for 20 minutes, or until a toothpick inserted in the center of a cupcake comes out clean or with a few crumbs. Cool the cupcakes completely on a wire rack before frosting them.

(continued)

PINEAPPLE MOJITO CUPCAKES

(CONTINUED)

FROSTING

1 cup (227 g) butter, room temperature

3 cups (360 g) confectioners' sugar

½ tsp vanilla extract

2 tbsp (30 ml) lime juice

2 tsp (4 g) lime zest

½ tsp mint leaves, minced, or ¼ tsp mint extract

Pinch of salt, optional

GARNISH

1 whole fresh pineapple (for the pineapple flowers)

Lime zest

Mint leaves

FOR THE FROSTING: Add the butter to a stand mixer or a large mixing bowl with a hand mixer. Beat until it is smooth. Add the confectioners' sugar, vanilla, lime juice, lime zest, minced mint leaves and salt, if using. Beat until incorporated.

FOR THE PINEAPPLE FLOWER GARNISH: Preheat the oven to 200°F (93°C). Cut the top and bottom off your pineapple with a sharp knife. Cut off the outer skin with a knife. Carefully remove as many of the eyes (dark spots) as you can from the pineapple using a knife or a melon baller. Do not cut into the pineapple excessively. Slice the pineapple as thinly as possible. Place the slices onto paper towels to remove most of the moisture. Continue to pat them with more paper towels to dry them.

Place the pineapple slices onto a parchment-lined baking pan. Bake for 1 hour. Turn each pineapple slice over and bake for 1 more hour. Remove the pineapple slices from the baking pan and place them into a cupcake pan. Press the centers of the pineapple slices into each cupcake well, so that the pineapples start to look like flowers. Let the slices finish drying overnight on the kitchen counter, uncovered.

ASSEMBLY: Use an apple corer or a knife to cut the center out of the cupcakes about three-quarters of the way down. Add the pineapple curd to a pastry bag and cut off the tip. Pipe the filling inside of the cupcake. Place the top back onto the cupcake.

Add the frosting to another pastry bag with a large round piping tip. Pipe the frosting on top of the cupcake in a circular motion. Garnish with lime zest, mint leaves and a pineapple flower.

PUMPKIN CREAM BRIOCHE DOUGHNUTS

SERVINGS:
12 TO 14 DOUGHNUTS

Nothing says fall like pumpkin! The pumpkin spice fever starts in August with pumpkin spice lattes, pumpkin cakes and everything else in between. The world can't wait for pumpkin season. So, let's break out the cozy sweaters and boots and enjoy these brioche doughnuts filled with silky pumpkin pastry cream and sprinkled with toasty glazed pumpkin seeds. These would be absolutely divine for a holiday brunch or tea, or any celebration happening in the fall.

DOUGHNUTS

1¾ cups (420 ml) milk

¼ cup (50 g) granulated sugar

1 tbsp (12 g) yeast

3 large eggs

1 tsp vanilla extract

1 tsp salt

2½ cups (313 g) all-purpose flour

2½ cups (343 g) bread flour

½ cup (114 g) butter, room temperature

67.7 fl oz (2 L) vegetable oil, for frying

FOR THE DOUGHNUTS: Warm the milk in the microwave to 110°F (43°C), for 50 to 60 seconds. Do not let it get hot, just lightly warmed. Stir together the warm milk, sugar and yeast in a stand mixer and let it sit for 10 minutes. Add the eggs, vanilla, salt, all-purpose flour and bread flour. Put on the dough hook attachment and let the dough mix until it is blended.

Add the butter one tablespoon (14 g) at a time until it is fully incorporated. Continue to allow the dough to knead for 2 minutes. Remove the bowl from the stand mixer. Cover the bowl with a towel and let the dough proof for 1½ to 2 hours. Transfer the dough to a smaller bowl, cover with plastic wrap and refrigerate overnight. Chilling the dough makes it easier to form the doughnuts.

The next day, divide the dough into twelve to fourteen equal pieces and roll each piece into a ball. Cut out parchment paper squares for each doughnut and place the doughnuts on top of them. This will make it easier to place them into the oil.

Add the oil to a large pot until it reaches halfway to the top. Heat the oil to between 360 and 375°F (182 and 191°C). Use a candy thermometer to get the exact temperature. Working in batches, gently place each doughnut into the oil using the parchment squares. Fry the doughnuts until they are golden brown, turning them once. Place a cooling rack on top of a baking pan. Remove the doughnuts from the oil and place on the cooling rack to drain and cool. Repeat with the remaining doughnuts.

(continued)

PUMPKIN CREAM BRIOCHE DOUGHNUTS

(CONTINUED)

GARNISH
1 cup (200 g) granulated sugar
2 tsp (4 g) cinnamon
Pumpkin seeds

PUMPKIN PASTRY CREAM
1 cup (240 ml) heavy cream
½ cup (120 ml) whole milk
¾ cup (150 g) granulated sugar, divided
2 tbsp (16 g) all-purpose flour
¼ tsp salt
4 large egg yolks
⅔ cups (162 g) canned pumpkin purée

FILLING
½ cup (120 ml) heavy cream
1 tsp granulated sugar
Prepared pumpkin pastry cream

FOR THE GARNISH: In a small dish, mix 1 cup (200 g) of granulated sugar and the cinnamon. Completely cover each doughnut with the cinnamon-sugar mixture. Place the sugared doughnuts on a baking sheet.

FOR THE PUMPKIN PASTRY CREAM: Warm the heavy cream and milk in a saucepan until it is very warm, right before it starts to boil.

In a medium bowl, whisk together the sugar, flour and salt. Add the egg yolks and pumpkin purée and whisk them into the dry ingredients. Pour a little of the hot liquid into the eggs and whisk; repeat the process until all of the liquid is poured into the eggs. When all the liquid has been added to the eggs, pour the mixture back into the saucepan. Set the pan back over medium heat. Whisk continuously until the mixture has thickened to a pudding-like consistency and is smooth. Remove from the heat and pour into an airtight container. Place into the refrigerator overnight or for at least 2 hours. When you are ready to use it, stir. If the mixture seems too thick, add a bit of milk into it and stir until it is smooth.

FOR THE FILLING: Add the heavy cream and sugar to a medium-sized bowl and beat the cream with a hand mixer until it forms stiff peaks. Fold the whipped cream into the prepared pumpkin pastry cream until it is incorporated.

ASSEMBLY: Use a knife or wooden spoon handle to make a hole in the side of each doughnut. Place the filling in a piping bag with a piping tip attached. Pipe the filling in each doughnut until it is filled. Top with pumpkin seeds.

STRAWBERRY HEART DOUGHNUTS

SERVINGS:
12 TO 14 DOUGHNUTS

Here's another soft, pillowy doughnut worthy of any celebration. These heart-shaped beauties start with a rich, buttery brioche dough, are fried to perfection, and are then filled with a rich, creamy strawberry pastry cream. They are finished with a dusting of crushed freeze-dried strawberries and granulated sugar. These decadent doughnuts are truly a strawberry dessert lover's dream!

DOUGHNUTS

1¾ cups (420 ml) milk

¼ cup (50 g) granulated sugar

1 tbsp (12 g) yeast

3 large eggs

1 tsp vanilla extract

1 tsp salt

2½ cups (313 g) all-purpose flour

2½ cups (343 g) bread flour

½ cup (114 g) butter, room temperature

67.7 fl oz (2 L) vegetable oil, for frying

FOR THE DOUGHNUTS: Warm the milk in the microwave to about 110°F (43°C), for 50 to 60 seconds. Do not let it get hot, just lightly warmed. Add the warm milk, sugar and yeast to a stand mixer and let it sit for 10 minutes. Add the eggs, vanilla, salt, all-purpose flour and bread flour. Put on the dough hook attachment and let the dough mix until blended.

Add the butter one tablespoon (14 g) at a time until it is fully incorporated. Continue to allow the dough to knead for 2 minutes. Remove the bowl from the stand mixer. Cover it with a towel and let the dough proof for 1½ to 2 hours. Transfer the dough to a smaller bowl, cover with plastic wrap and refrigerate overnight.

The next day, roll out the dough on a lightly floured surface until it's ½ to ¾ inch (1.5 to 2 cm) thick. Use a 2- or 2½-inch (5- or 6-cm) heart-shaped cookie cutter to cut out twelve to fourteen doughnuts. Cut out parchment paper squares and place the doughnuts on top of them. This will make it easier to place them into the oil.

Add the oil to a large pot until it reaches halfway to the top. Heat the oil to between 360 and 375°F (182 and 191°C). Use a candy thermometer to get the exact temperature. Working in batches, gently place each doughnut into the oil using the parchment squares. Fry the doughnuts until they are golden brown, turning them once. Place a cooling rack on top of a baking pan. Remove the doughnuts from the oil and place them on the cooling rack to drain and cool. In between batches, prepare the garnish to coat the warm doughnuts. Repeat with the remaining doughnuts.

(continued)

STRAWBERRY HEART DOUGHNUTS

(CONTINUED)

GARNISH
1 cup (200 g) granulated sugar
¼ cup (5 g) freeze-dried strawberries

STRAWBERRY PASTRY CREAM
2 cups (288 g) whole strawberries
1 cup (240 ml) heavy cream
½ cup (120 ml) whole milk
¾ cup (150 g) granulated sugar
2 tbsp (16 g) all-purpose flour
¼ tsp salt
4 large egg yolks

FILLING
½ cup (240 ml) heavy cream
1 tsp granulated sugar
Prepared Strawberry Pastry Cream

FOR THE GARNISH: While the doughnuts are frying, in a food processor, add the sugar and freeze-dried strawberries. Blend until all of the strawberries are crushed. While the doughnuts are still warm, sprinkle each of them on both sides with the strawberry-sugar mixture. Place the sugared doughnuts on a baking sheet.

FOR THE STRAWBERRY PASTRY CREAM: Add the strawberries to a high-powered blender and blend on high until the purée is smooth. Strain the strawberry purée through a fine-mesh strainer into a bowl. Cover the bowl and set aside.

Warm the heavy cream and milk in a saucepan until it is very warm, right before it starts to boil. In a medium-sized bowl, whisk together the sugar, flour and salt. Add the egg yolks and 1 cup (312 g) of the strawberry purée and whisk them into the dry ingredients. Pour a little of the hot liquid into the eggs and whisk; repeat the process until all of the liquid is poured into the eggs. When all the liquid has been added to the eggs, pour the mixture back into the saucepan. Set the pan back over medium heat. Whisk continuously until the mixture has thickened to a pudding-like consistency and is smooth. Remove the pan from the heat and pour into an airtight container. Place the pastry cream into the refrigerator overnight or for 2 hours. When you are ready to use it, stir. If the mixture seems too thick, add a bit of milk into it and stir until smooth.

FOR THE FILLING: Add the heavy cream and sugar to a medium-sized bowl and beat the cream with a hand mixer until there are stiff peaks. Fold the whipped cream into the strawberry pastry cream until it is incorporated.

ASSEMBLY: Use a knife or wooden spoon handle to make a hole in the back or bottom of each doughnut (so the hole will not be visible and the heart shape will not be distorted). Place the filling in a piping bag with a piping tip attached. Pipe the filling in each doughnut until it is filled. Sprinkle with additional strawberry-sugar mixture, if desired.

BLOOD ORANGE ROSEMARY CUPCAKES

**SERVINGS:
12 TO 14 CUPCAKES**

I recently became totally obsessed with blood oranges. That crimson-red color is just absolutely gorgeous—not to mention how beautiful they photograph when sliced in half. Blood oranges are less tangy than standard oranges and have more of a floral or tart flavor. They're also called raspberry oranges because of their taste. These cupcakes have a rich blood orange pastry cream in the center and also in the frosting, with a hint of savory rosemary.

BLOOD ORANGE CURD

4 large egg yolks

⅓ cup (66 g) granulated sugar

1 tbsp (6 g) blood orange zest

⅓ cup (80 ml) freshly squeezed blood orange juice

1 tbsp (8 g) cornstarch

2 tbsp (30 ml) heavy cream

¼ cup + 2 tbsp (84 g) butter

CUPCAKES

2 large eggs, room temperature

1 cup (200 g) granulated sugar

2 tbsp (28 g) butter, room temperature

¼ cup (60 ml) vegetable oil

1 tsp vanilla extract

2 tsp (10 ml) blood orange juice

2 tsp (4 g) blood orange zest

¼ cup (60 ml) buttermilk, room temperature

¼ cup (60 ml) sour cream, room temperature

1½ cups (188 g) all-purpose flour

1½ tsp (7 g) baking powder

½ tsp baking soda

½ tsp salt

2 tsp (2 g) chopped rosemary

FOR THE BLOOD ORANGE CURD: In a small saucepan, place the egg yolks, sugar, blood orange zest, blood orange juice, cornstarch and heavy cream; whisk by hand to combine. Cook over low to medium heat for 5 to 10 minutes, whisking constantly, until the mixture becomes thick.

Remove the curd from the heat and immediately strain it through a fine-mesh sieve over a bowl by pushing the curd through with a spoon or rubber spatula. Discard any small pieces of cooked egg left in the sieve. Add the butter and whisk it into the curd until it's completely melted. Place the curd in an airtight container and refrigerate it for at least 2 hours or overnight.

FOR THE CUPCAKES: Preheat the oven to 350°F (177°C). Line a twelve-cup muffin pan with paper liners. And two additional liners to another muffin pan if making more than twelve.

In a stand mixer with the paddle attachment or a large mixing bowl with a hand mixer, add the eggs and sugar. Beat for 2 minutes, or until thick and fluffy. Add the butter and oil, and then mix again. Add the vanilla, blood orange juice, blood orange zest, buttermilk and sour cream, and blend together. Add in the flour, baking powder, baking soda, salt and chopped rosemary and blend until smooth.

(continued)

BLOOD ORANGE ROSEMARY CUPCAKES

(CONTINUED)

FROSTING
1 cup (227 g) butter, room temperature

3 cups (360 g) confectioners' sugar

Pinch of kosher salt

½ tsp vanilla extract

2 tbsp (30 ml) blood orange juice

2 tsp (4 g) blood orange zest

GARNISH
Freeze-dried blood orange slices

Rosemary sprigs

Scoop the batter into the pan, filling the wells halfway to three-quarters full. Bake for 20 minutes, or until a toothpick inserted in the center of a cupcake comes out clean or with a few crumbs. Cool completely on a wire rack before frosting.

FOR THE FROSTING: Add the butter to a stand mixer or a large mixing bowl with a hand mixer. Beat until smooth. Add the confectioners' sugar, salt and vanilla. Mix until everything is incorporated. Add the blood orange juice and blood orange zest. Beat until everything is incorporated.

ASSEMBLY: Use an apple corer or a knife to cut the center out of each cupcake about three-quarters of the way down. Add the blood orange curd to a pastry bag and cut off the tip. Pipe the filling inside of the cupcake. Place the top of the removed cake back onto the cupcake.

Add the frosting to another pastry bag fitted with a large star tip. Pipe the frosting on top of the cupcake in a circular motion. Repeat with the remaining cupcakes. Garnish with freeze-dried blood orange slices and rosemary sprigs.

NOTE: Look for freeze-dried blood oranges online, such as on Amazon; they are available by many companies, and may be called freeze-dried cocktail garnishes. If freeze-dried blood oranges are unavailable, you can use thin slices of fresh blood oranges to garnish instead.

LEMON TEA CAKES

SERVINGS: 12 TEA CAKES

While these are called tea cakes, they really can be eaten anytime and at any celebration! Serve them when friends and family come over or at springtime gatherings such as Easter, Mother's Day or even a baby or bridal shower.

TEA CAKES

1 large egg, room temperature

⅔ cup (132 g) granulated sugar

½ cup (120 ml) olive oil

1 tsp vanilla extract

½–1 tsp chopped thyme

2 tsp (4 g) lemon zest

3 tbsp (45 ml) lemon juice

1½ cups (180 g) cake flour

2 tsp (9 g) baking powder

¼ tsp salt

½ cup (120 ml) buttermilk, room temperature

GLAZE

1 cup (120 g) confectioners' sugar

2 tsp (10 ml) heavy cream

4 tsp (20 ml) fresh lemon juice

GARNISH

Lemon wedges

Thyme sprigs

FOR THE TEA CAKES: Preheat the oven to 350°F (177°C). Spray a 12-cup muffin pan with baking spray.

In a stand mixer with the paddle attachment or a large mixing bowl with a hand mixer, add the egg and granulated sugar. Beat the mixture until it is thick and fluffy, for 2 minutes. Mix in the olive oil. Add the vanilla, chopped thyme, lemon zest and lemon juice. Mix well. Add the cake flour, baking powder, salt and buttermilk and mix until everything is combined. Divide the batter among the wells of the muffin pan.

Bake for 25 to 30 minutes. Allow the tea cakes to cool completely on a wire rack.

FOR THE GLAZE: Mix the confectioners' sugar, heavy cream and lemon juice in a bowl until evenly combined and smooth.

Cut off the dome of each cake, so that they are leveled. Turn the cakes upside down and place them on a platter. Spoon a tablespoon of glaze on top of each cake. Garnish with a lemon wedge and a sprig of thyme.

VANILLA CAKE POPS

SERVINGS:
12 TO 14 CAKE POPS

Cake pops are the cutest desserts on a stick! There are so many ways to make and decorate them, from the simplest design to the most elaborate. There wouldn't be a themed birthday party without them. Leave them with just a chocolate outer coating, add a few sprinkles or add a few fondant flowers to them. There are so many ways to make them beautiful.

1 large egg + 1 large egg white, room temperature

¾ cup (150 g) granulated sugar

¼ cup + 2 tbsp (90 ml) vegetable oil

2 tsp (10 ml) vanilla extract

¾ cup (180 ml) buttermilk, room temperature

1¼ cups (156 g) all-purpose flour

2 tsp (9 g) baking powder

½ tsp baking soda

¼ tsp salt

1 tbsp (17 g) vanilla frosting (can frosting)

1 (12-oz [340-g]) bag white candy melts

1 tbsp (12 g) paramount crystals or (15 ml) vegetable oil

12–14 cake pop sticks or straws

Pink food gel or food coloring

1 box of white fondant

Shortening, for rolling out fondant

FOR THE CAKE: Preheat the oven to 350°F (177°C). Line a 9 × 13–inch (23 × 33–cm) pan with parchment paper.

In a stand mixer with the paddle attachment or a large mixing bowl with a hand mixer, add the egg, egg white and sugar. Beat for 2 minutes, until the mixture is thick and fluffy. Add the oil, and then mix again. Add the vanilla and buttermilk. Mix together. Add the flour, baking powder, baking soda and salt and mix until smooth.

Pour the batter evenly into the prepared pan. Bake the cake for 25 to 35 minutes or until the top is lightly browned. Remove the cake from the oven to cool completely.

ASSEMBLY: Cut away all of the browned outside layer of the cake. In a large bowl, crumble the cake with your hands. Add the frosting to the crumbled cake, mix it in and knead the cake dough with your hands until the frosting is evenly incorporated.

Use a cookie scoop to scoop even amounts of cake balls from the mixture. Shape the cake into balls by rolling the dough between the palms of your hands in a circular motion. Place the cake balls onto a small baking sheet and place the sheet into the refrigerator until ready to use.

(continued)

VANILLA CAKE POPS

(CONTINUED)

Pour the bag of candy melts into a microwave-safe bowl. Add the paramount crystals. Microwave the candy melts for 60 seconds. Remove and stir continuously. Not all of the candy melts will be melted, but most of them will be. If the mixture is not fully melted, place the bowl back in and microwave in 30-second intervals, stopping and stirring between each interval until the mixture is fully melted.

Dip the tip of each cake pop stick into the melted candy and poke it inside a cake ball about halfway through. Place the dipped cake pops back onto the baking sheet and transfer them to the refrigerator for 10 minutes.

Pour the melted candy into a tall narrow cup. Dip each cake pop into the cup and make sure the entire cake pop is covered. Slowly pull the cake pop out of the mixture. Tap the cake pop on the side of the cup a few times to remove extra melted candy. Stand the cake pops on a parchment-lined baking sheet.

Add a couple drops of pink food gel/coloring to the fondant. Knead the color into the fondant. It does not have to blend in all of the way; there can be streaks of white and pink.

Take a small amount of fondant and press it into differently shaped flower silicone molds. Remove the fondant flowers and place them in the freezer for 10 minutes.

Lightly cover a cutting board with shortening. Roll out more of the fondant. Use flower fondant cutters/plungers to make more flowers.

Remelt or melt more candy melts, and use a bit of the melted candy to glue the different fondant flowers to the cake pops.

RASPBERRY WHITE CHOCOLATE MACARONS

**SERVINGS:
36 TO 48 MACARONS**

Macarons . . . the French traditional meringue and almond cookie that's so beautiful and delicious. These cookies are known to be a little tricky to make, but they are definitely achievable. I mean, can we even have a wedding shower or baby shower without them? And these macarons have a raspberry white chocolate center that is unbelievably delicious.

MACARONS

1 cup + 2 tsp (100 g) almond flour

1¼ cups (150 g) confectioners' sugar

3 large egg whites, room temperature

½ cup (100 g) granulated sugar

¼ tsp cream of tartar

Pinch of salt

1 tsp vanilla extract

Pink/red food gel

FOR THE MACARONS: Weigh the almond flour and confectioners' sugar for the most correct measurements and to ensure success with your macarons. Add the almond flour and confectioners' sugar to a bowl. Sift them together into a second bowl to get rid of any large pieces. Do not skip this step. Set this aside.

In a stand mixer with a whisk attachment or a large bowl with a hand mixer, whip the egg whites. As the egg whites start foaming, add the granulated sugar 1 tablespoon (15 g) at a time and continue whipping. Add the cream of tartar and salt and whip more until the mixture is glossy and stiff. You should be able to hold the bowl upside down without the meringue sliding out. Add the vanilla and pink/red food gel and whip just until the vanilla and the color is incorporated. Remove the bowl from the stand mixer.

Fold the dry mixture into the meringue using a rubber spatula until the mixture holds a 10 count. This means that when the batter falls from the spatula to the bowl, it takes about 10 seconds until it fully blends into the rest of the batter. This takes approximately 45 turns. Do not over mix!

Fit a pastry bag with a 1A tip and place the pastry bag in a tall glass, flipping the outside of the bag over the rim of the glass. Fill the piping bag with the macaron batter.

Place three silicone mats with macaron patterns or parchment paper on three 12 × 17–inch (30 × 43–cm) baking sheets.

(continued)

RASPBERRY WHITE CHOCOLATE MACARONS

(CONTINUED)

RASPBERRY WHITE CHOCOLATE GANACHE

¾ cup (92 g) raspberries, fresh or frozen

2 tbsp (30 g) granulated sugar

1½ cups (360 g) white chocolate chips

Pipe 1-inch (2.5-cm) rounds of batter onto the baking sheets, spacing them at least 1 inch (2.5 cm) apart. Tap the baking sheets hard on the countertop four to five times to release trapped air, and then let them sit at room temperature for 30 minutes to an hour, or until the unbaked macarons form a skin and do not stick to your finger when touched.

Preheat the oven to 300°F (149°C). Bake for 14 minutes on the center rack, one pan at a time. Cool the macarons completely on a cooling rack.

FOR THE RASPBERRY WHITE CHOCOLATE GANACHE: Add the raspberries and sugar to a medium-sized saucepan. Bring it to a full boil and cook for about 5 to 8 minutes. Remove the saucepan from heat. Pour the hot mixture into a blender and purée until it is smooth. Strain the mixture to remove the seeds. While the purée is still hot, whisk the white chocolate chips into the purée until it is smooth. Refrigerate the ganache to set for at least 1 hour or overnight.

ASSEMBLY: Place the raspberry ganache in a piping bag. Cut off about 1 inch from the tip and pipe the ganache on one macaron shell. Sandwich it with another macaron shell. Continue with remaining macaron shells until all the shells have been filled.

BANANA CARAMEL PETIT FOURS

SERVINGS:
15 TO 18 PETIT FOURS

Petit fours are a classic dessert. I made this version using a moist banana cake with caramel buttercream and a little extra caramel drip. Bananas and caramel are a great combo and pairing them together in this easy dessert makes it a hit that your guests will love!

BANANA CAKE

½ cup (114 g) butter, room temperature

1 cup (200 g) granulated sugar

2 large eggs, room temperature

1 cup (240 ml) sour cream, room temperature

1 tsp vanilla extract

2 cups (250 g) all-purpose flour

2 tsp (9 g) baking powder

½ tsp baking soda

½ tsp salt

1 cup (225 g) mashed bananas, about 3 overripe bananas

CARAMEL BUTTERCREAM

1 cup (227 g) unsalted butter, room temperature

3–4 cups (480 g) confectioners' sugar

2 tsp (10 ml) vanilla extract

½ cup (120 ml) jarred salted caramel

Pinch of salt

GARNISH

1 banana, sliced

Additional salted caramel

Chopped walnuts

FOR THE CAKE: Preheat the oven to 350°F (177°C). Line a 9 × 13–inch (23 × 33–cm) baking pan with parchment paper.

In a stand mixer with the paddle attachment or a large bowl with a hand mixer, cream the butter and granulated sugar together until it is light and fluffy. Add the eggs and beat again. Mix in the sour cream and vanilla. Mix until everything is combined. Add the flour, baking powder, baking soda and salt. Mix on medium speed until combined. Stir in the mashed bananas.

Spoon the batter into the prepared pan evenly. Bake the cake for 25 to 35 minutes or until the top is lightly browned. Remove from the oven to allow the cake to cool completely.

FOR THE CARAMEL BUTTERCREAM: In a stand mixer fitted with the paddle attachment or a large bowl with a hand mixer, whip the butter on high for 5 to 6 minutes, until it's fluffy. Scrape down the bowl a few times as needed. Add the confectioners' sugar a few cups at a time as the frosting mixes. Add the vanilla and salted caramel. Add the salt and beat for a few more minutes. Refrigerate the caramel buttercream until ready to use.

ASSEMBLY: Use a 2- or 2½-inch (5- or 6-cm) cookie or biscuit cutter to cut out circles from the cake. Slice each cake round in half horizontally. Place the caramel buttercream in a piping bag. Pipe a swirl of buttercream on the bottom half. Add the top half and pipe another swirl of buttercream. Add a piece of sliced banana. Drizzle on some salted caramel, and then sprinkle on the chopped walnuts. Repeat with the remaining cakes.

HUMMINGBIRD MINI BUNDTS

SERVINGS: 12 MINI BUNDTS

Hummingbird cake is a traditional southern cake, but it first originated in Jamaica. It's a moist cake filled with banana, pineapples and spices and is so good! I've made this amazing cake into a mini form and gave it a nice glaze. You'll want to serve these to all of your family and friends, and they will be smitten with the adorable mini version of this beloved cake.

CAKE

1 cup (109 g) chopped pecans

3 large eggs, room temperature

1½ cups (300 g) granulated sugar

⅔ cup (160 ml) vegetable oil

1½ tsp (7 ml) vanilla extract

1½ cups (338 g) ripe bananas, mashed (about 4 large bananas)

1 (8-oz [227-ml]) can crushed pineapple (do not drain)

2½ cups (313 g) all-purpose flour

1 tsp baking soda

2 tsp (9 g) baking powder

1 tsp cinnamon

½ tsp salt

GLAZE

4 oz (114 g) cream cheese, cubed and brought to room temperature

2 cups (240 g) sifted confectioners' sugar

1 tsp vanilla extract

1–2 tbsp (15–30 ml) milk, divided

GARNISH

Chopped pecans

FOR THE CAKE: Preheat the oven to 350°F (177°C). Place the chopped pecans in an even layer on a parchment-lined baking pan. Bake for 6 to 8 minutes or until toasted, stirring halfway through. Remove the pecans from the oven and set them aside.

In a stand mixer with a paddle attachment or a large bowl with a hand mixer, beat the eggs and granulated sugar until lightened. Add the oil, vanilla, mashed bananas and can of crushed pineapples with the juice, and mix again on low speed. Add the flour, baking soda, baking powder, cinnamon and salt. Mix until incorporated. Gently stir in the toasted pecans.

Spray two mini-Bundt pans with baking spray. Place the batter in the pans, filling each mini Bundt well about three-quarters full with batter. Bake for 20 to 25 minutes, until a toothpick inserted in a Bundt comes out clean or with a few crumbs. Cool the mini Bundts completely on a wire rack.

FOR THE GLAZE: In a stand mixer or a medium bowl with a hand mixer, add the cream cheese, confectioners' sugar, vanilla and 1 tablespoon (15 ml) of milk. Beat until smooth. Add additional milk, 1 teaspoon at a time, until it gets to your desired consistency.

Spoon the glaze over the mini Bundt cakes, and sprinkle with additional chopped pecans.

NOTE: Each mini-Bundt pan should make six mini Bundts. If you only have one pan, bake the batter in batches.

WHITE CHOCOLATE PEPPERMINT MERINGUE COOKIES

SERVINGS: 6 TO 7 DOZEN

Meringue is a versatile, beautiful dessert made from whipping egg whites and sugar. And if you pipe the meringue on a baking sheet and bake it on a low temperature for a while, you will create a lovely cookie! These cookies are perfect for the holidays. After they bake, dip them in a little white chocolate and roll them in crushed peppermint candy. These will definitely get you on the nice list!

3 large egg whites, cold

Pinch of salt

¾ cup (150 g) superfine granulated sugar

¼ tsp cream of tartar

½ tsp vanilla extract

5 (140 g) peppermint candy canes

2 (3.5-oz [98-g]) high-quality white chocolate bars

1 tsp vegetable oil

NOTE: If you can't find superfine sugar, blend granulated sugar in a food processor or blender until it's a very fine consistency.

FOR THE MERINGUE: Preheat the oven to 200°F (93°C). Add the egg whites, salt, sugar and cream of tartar to the bowl on a stand mixer. Whisk together until everything is fully combined.

Fill a small pot with about 2 inches (5 cm) of water and bring it to a simmer. Set the bowl of the stand mixer over the pot of simmering water. Constantly whisk the mixture for 3 to 5 minutes until the egg whites reach 160°F (71°C) and the sugar has dissolved. Remove the bowl from the heat and attach the bowl to a stand mixer fitted with a whisk attachment. Turn the mixer on, and gradually increase the speed until it reaches medium-high. You can also do this step with a hand mixer. Add in the vanilla and whip the meringue for 8 minutes, until it is glossy, begins to thicken and gets stiff peaks.

Add the meringue to a pastry bag fitted with a large star tip. Pipe 1-inch (2.5-cm) meringues onto a parchment-lined baking sheet. Bake for 1 hour. After 1 hour, turn the oven off and keep them in the oven for 1 additional hour. Let the meringues cool completely.

ASSEMBLY: Add the peppermint candy canes to a ziplock bag or food processor and crush them finely. Set aside.

Add the white chocolate bars to a heatproof bowl. Place the bowl over a small saucepan filled one-third full with boiling water, making sure the bottom of the bowl does not touch the water. Stir the white chocolate with a rubber spatula until it is fully melted. Mix in the oil, and then remove the bowl from the heat.

Dip the bottom of each meringue cookie into the white chocolate, and then immediately dip it into the crushed peppermints. Place the meringue cookies on a parchment-lined baking sheet to set.

CITRUS MADELEINES

SERVINGS: 24 MADELEINES

The first time I had a madeleine was at a French restaurant in Harlem called Chez Lucienne French Bistro. After dinner, the waiter came by with a basket of these warm little cakes. When I bit into one for the first time, I was in absolute heaven! I knew I had to try making these light buttery creations at home. After experimenting with many recipes over the years, this version has become my go-to. They are absolutely magnifique!

MADELEINES

3 large eggs, room temperature

⅔ cup (132 g) granulated sugar

1¼ cups (156 g) all-purpose flour

2 tsp (4 g) lemon zest

2 tsp (4 g) lime zest

½ cup (114 g) unsalted butter, melted

Additional melted butter for the molds

GLAZE

¾ cup (150 g) confectioners' sugar

1 tbsp (15 ml) lemon juice

1 tbsp (15 ml) lime juice

1 tbsp (15 ml) water

FOR THE MADELEINES: In a stand mixer with a paddle attachment or a large bowl with a hand mixer, beat the eggs and granulated sugar for 6 minutes, until the mixture is thick and pale.

Spoon the flour into a sifter or fine-mesh sieve. Use a rubber spatula to fold the flour into the batter as you sift it over the bowl.

Add the lemon and lime zest and slowly spoon the butter into the batter, a few spoonfuls at a time, folding the batter as you add it in. Cover the bowl and refrigerate it for 12 hours or overnight.

About 1 hour before you are ready to bake, brush two madeleine pans with melted butter, and then dust it with a bit of flour. Place it into the freezer until ready to use.

Preheat the oven to 425°F (218°C). Spoon the batter into the first madeleine pan, filling the wells about three-quarters full. Bake for 8 to 9 minutes or until the cakes feel and look set. Repeat with the second pan.

FOR THE GLAZE: In a small mixing bowl, stir together the confectioners' sugar, lemon juice, lime juice and water until the mixture is smooth.

Remove the madeleines from the oven and place them on a cooling rack. While they are still warm, dip each cake in the glaze, and place them back on the cooking rack, scalloped side up. Allow the cakes to sit until they have cooled and the glaze has firmed up.

ACKNOWLEDGMENTS

Getting the opportunity to create this incredible cookbook has been so amazing.

I'd like to thank Sarah Monroe and the entire team at Page Street Publishing for giving me this incredible opportunity. Thank you for your support and guidance with this amazing project. You and your team definitely made my dream come to life.

To my husband, Freddy, for all of your support and honesty with my recipes and with my food photography.

To my amazing children, Julian and Layla, for being the best taste testers and letting me know what tastes great and what should and should not be included in this book.

Thank you to my amazing mother who is my hero, my role model, my everything. Without your love, encouragement and help, I would not exist. And I would also like to thank my parents for testing my recipes, giving me great feedback and watching the kids for me when I had to get this book done.

To my sister-in-law Emily—thank you so much for being there for me from the very beginning of me creating my Peaches 2 Peaches blog. You have been my number one supporter, and you have always encouraged me to keep going and keep putting everything I had into this, especially when I felt like giving up at times.

To my sister-in-law Lizette, who was instrumental in helping me come up with recipe ideas and helping me brainstorm when I felt "stuck."

To Nery, for the numerous pep talks and encouragement to always "go big" and strive for the best.

To Aunt Cherie, who has always been a huge supporter of me and my work. You have always told me and everyone around you how proud you were of me and that means the world to me.

To my Uncle Bob for being an amazing father figure to me my whole life and who always encouraged me when I needed it.

To my GSS family: Jesus, Betsy, Toni, Donna, Naida, Cleo, Angelica, Naja, Wendy P, Wendy T, Leann, Lauren G and Antonio, for always being my forever taste testers and always encouraging me to pursue my dreams of baking.

I have met, virtually and in person, so many amazing individuals on social media who have become great friends over the past few years. To my amazing Food Capture Collective family: Angela, Kirby, Doaa, Dora, Ashley, Larisa, Anu, Savya, Katie and Nina. I can't imagine what my food blogging and food photography journey would have been without you guys. All of your support, help, encouragement and advice has been just priceless!

To Eva Kosmas Flores, for listening to me and giving me amazing advice during this book writing journey.

To my lovely literary agent, Felice Laverne, thank you for bringing me into your agency and all of your support and help with navigating me through this whole process.

To my amazing grandmother, who I hold in my heart, and who has been my baking inspiration for everything that I do.

And lastly, to my amazing supporters and followers of Peaches 2 Peaches. Thank you for following along with me through my food blogging journey.

ABOUT THE AUTHOR

Monique McLeod-Polanco is a food blogger and food photographer. Peaches 2 Peaches is an homage to her grandmother who was known for her southern peach cobbler. She has a master's degree in social work and worked for several years as a high school social worker before starting her blog and food photography business.

Her work has been featured in feedfeed, *Bake from Scratch*, MyRecipes and Kitchn. She currently resides in New York with her family.

INDEX